INCREASE YOUR FAITH

PRACTICAL STEPS TO BELIEVE FOR THE IMPOSSIBLE

STEVE BREMNER

Illustrated by
JOSE ALJOVIN

Copyright 2013 © by Steve Bremner

Fire Press Publications

ISBN-13: 978-1491268896

All rights reserved

No portion of this work may be reproduced or quoted from at length except if a link is provided back to the page where this book is sold and the author's name must be mentioned with the quote.

If you wish to use an excerpt that is longer than 500 words for the purposes of review in a blog or website, please contact the author for personal permission explaining your intent. The only reason for this is that Amazon.com has a very strict copyright policy about portions of publications enrolled in their Kindle Direct Program appearing freely on the internet. The author wishes to avoid any hassle.

Thank you for your understanding.

Unless otherwise indicated, all Scripture references are from The Holy Bible, English Standard Version (ESV) Copyright © 2001 by Crossway, a publishing ministry of Good News Publishers. Used by permission. All rights reserved.

It is rare to find a perfect book, but in this day and age of digital books and print-on-demand publishing, we can correct our mistakes rather quickly. If you find a typo or error in this book, we'd be extremely grateful if you would drop us an email to let us know.

Contact us at fireonyourhead@stevebremner.com

CONTENTS

Preface	v
Introduction: Looking at Abraham	1
Faith Is Not Mental	9
Faith For the Impossible	21
Why Study Faith?	39
Believe That You Have Received It	49
Is Mustard Seed Really Enough to Speak to the Mountains in Your Life?	59
Growing Deeper Roots	69
Understanding Confession	95
About the Author	107
Fire On Your Head Podcast	111
Also by Steve Bremner	113
Get These Bonuses When You Buy Our Audiobook	117
Partner With Us As Missionaries	123

PREFACE

This is technically the third edition of *Increase Your Faith*. I originally released the second edition of the Kindle book only a few months after the first edition came out one month after my first book, *6 Lies People Believe About Divine Healing*.

In early 2011, before I ever bought my first Kindle device, I worked on a manuscript that was initially going to cover the subject of divine healing. The content in this e-book and *6 Lies About Healing* were both contained therein, but I struggled with how to make the subjects flow together in a coherent way. I was originally going to make a book with sections, in which one covered the lies people believe, and then the other section covered ways to grow in our faith to be able to see healing in our lives and ministries. That's when I discovered that with Kindle books there are literally no rules as to how long or short a book could be. People release "bite-sized" e-books all the time. I then prayerfully decided it was best to split the manuscript in half and make separate, shorter works.

I decided to make divine healing the subject of my first book, and focus on just demolishing lies people believe. The intended audience for that book is the child of God who thinks they're suffering to glorify God. As a result, I decided to put faith building and inspiration into another work altogether and make the subject more broad as believers have as many different needs as there are believers to have them. For some it may be a healing in their body, and for another it could be a struggle to believe God will provide finances to pay their electric bill.

The end result was this book. The difference between the healing book and this faith book is that I wrote this one to minister primarily to *myself*. I love writing. I love having revelations and teachings from the Lord flowing through my fingertips on to my computer screen. I love blogging, and my wife and mother of my two children has told me I need to pull myself away from the computer since I can easily spend hours in front of my screen writing and neglect the world, and my family, around me. Sometimes writing brings me peace.

So, it's my hope that my writings can bring other people peace as well as personal and spiritual challenge.

PREFACE

A lot of what you will read in this book was content I placed on my blog nearly a decade prior, but I've re-worked and re-edited the content tremendously as a way of building my own faith so that I could trust God to bring in thousands of dollars to help me pay for my wedding in May 2013. I didn't get nearly the amount of sales as I had hoped for from these two books, but God surprised us with many unexpected gifts and blessings as well as un-asked for offerings, and other intangible benefits that came from publishing Kindle books. This all helped us to not only avoid going into debt to pay for our wedding, but also allowing us to go on our honeymoon without borrowing any funds. Praise God!

I want you to know that I put into practice what I preach, and that is what has birthed this book, more so than 6 *Lies About Healing* in which I shared my motives for writing that book in its introduction. I figured if the things I mention have been good enough to help me out in my faith walk, then with my writing and narration skills I could hopefully help and bless others as well. I have made several changes in this book that didn't originally appear in the original e-book and print versions. I've included a few more testimonies early in the book, mostly of God providing finances for me on the mission field and more recent testimonies that have happened since the original version was released. I've also included few more

PREFACE

practical tips later on in the book to help grow deeper spiritual roots.

With that being said, it is my prayer that this book be but one of many tools you can add to your spiritual tool belt in order to grow in Christ.

Blessings and fire on your head,
Steve Bremner
August 7th, 2017

INTRODUCTION: LOOKING AT ABRAHAM

Thank you for picking up this book. You obviously desire to increase your faith. Whatever your motives for reading, it's my prayer that when you've finished, you'll be stirred up and inspired in your faith. That you will have had your mind changed about a few things.

This book is intended to be a companion to my other book, *6 Lies People Believe About Divine Healing*, which covers similar ground as you'll find here. If you liked that book and want to increase in your faith, then you're in luck as this book is designed to do just that.

Let's begin a book about faith by first looking at the life of one of the first figures in the Bible who is spoken of as having faith: Abraham.

> As it is written, "I have made you the father of many nations" — in the presence of the God in whom he believed, who gives life to the dead and calls into existence the things that do not exist.
> **In hope he believed against hope**, that he should become the father of many nations, as he had been told, "So shall your offspring be."
> **He did not weaken in faith** when he considered his own body, which was as good as dead (since he was about a hundred years old), or when he considered the barrenness of Sarah's womb.
> **No distrust made him waver** concerning the promise of God, but **he grew strong in his faith** as he gave glory to God,
> **fully convinced** that God was able to do what he had promised.
> That is why his faith was "counted to him as righteousness." (*Romans 4:17-22, emphasis mine*)

Listen to this testimony about Abraham. Paul wrote *he didn't waver in his faith*. Is that really true? I want to show you something interesting. Recall with me, if you will, that in the fifteenth chapter of Genesis Abram and his wife Sarai were promised the child Isaac, but it was roughly 25 years before the child of promise was born. In the next chapter Sarah grew weary of waiting for that promise to be fulfilled, so she gave her maid Hagar to Abram to bear a child with her.

Abraham *wavered* not? Did *not weaken in faith*? Is it true that no distrust made him waver? Did the apostle Paul actually *read* the story of Genesis? Oh, he did alright, and he caught on to something I didn't necessarily notice until recently. When God looked at Abraham's life, He saw a man of faith. He didn't zero-in on the 25 year span of time of waiting, and cancel out Abraham's faith after what happened with Ishmael. The Lord ultimately saw a man of faith in the big picture. Galatians 3:6 says that Abraham believed God, and it was counted to him as righteousness. Praise God that He looks at the cry of our heart instead of just the last mistake we made or doubt we acted on!

We can learn from the life of Abraham at least two things. First, Abraham clearly didn't *begin* with "great" faith to see the promise come about. His faith *grew* or his heart was changed over time.

Second, could it be said that *we ourselves* are in charge of how long it takes *for us to believe* the promises of God? Can our faith —or lack of it — accelerate or slow down the process of receiving the promises we've been given? Yes.

Romans 4:20 states that Abraham *grew strong in his faith.* If you can *grow strong* in your faith, then evidently you can stay weak and not grow at all in faith. I've taught that faith is like a seed and we are in charge of watering it ourselves. God gives a seed of faith — so to speak — to each one of us, and some people have greater faith, not because God gave them *greater* faith but because they've taken more time to grow *their* seed. Others keep their seed small, thinking, "God will only do what God wills", and these believers take no initiative of their own to believe for greater things. People get angry when they're told this, but if all it took to move mountains was faith that stayed the size of a mustard seed, then we would have moved all of our mountains already.

Keep in mind the parable of the sower (in Matthew 13:1-9). In each instance the seed is planted and goes into the soil, but for various reasons like shallow soil or weeds choking it out, the result is the plant is unfruitful. However, the one that takes root in good soil is up to a hundred times more fruitful than its initial form. Which is easier for the devil to steal — a *seed* or a *tree*? I hope you answered "tree". That wasn't a trick question. That is why we must water our seeds so they grow and become established, being careful also of what kind of soil we're planting in. The conditions of our hearts and minds are important. It is with this framework we're going to proceed and talk about how to water this seed, cultivate the soil of our hearts, and grow in our faith.

Could it be possible that Abraham is a man of whom it took twenty-five years to reach the place where his faith was strong enough to finally receive the promised son? I know some listeners will totally object. Some believe everything is based on the sovereignty of God which would, of necessity cancel out our actions and decisions. But God's sovereignty is just one side of a double-sided coin, and it seems way too many believers only accept one of either sides. But that's for another book.

There's a difference between how far a car will go on a full tank of gas, and how far it will go if the tank is empty. So it is with our faith — are you full or running on empty?

Faith is not believing that if you sit in a chair it will hold your weight. Maybe some of you listening need *hope* that the chair you're sitting in will hold your weight! Faith is not mental, it's the *action* of going ahead and sitting in that chair *knowing* you can.

Let's also look specifically at the things highlighted in our selected passage:

Do we *believe* God (v. 17)? I don't mean belief as a mental assent to what the Bible says. Believing the Bible is like the "entry level" faith. Do we *live* beyond the mental agreement like it is *real*? Is it normal to our lifestyle and beliefs that "He gives life to that which is dead", spiritual and physical (v.17)? Do we *know* and not just *think* that through Him, that which does not exist can be brought to existence?

This next statement is one that rocks me when comparing it to my life: *Belief against hope* (v.18). What does this mean and look like exactly? Remember, Sarah wasn't the only one that was barren — *they were both old*, and in Genesis 18 when the three angels came to tell Abraham they'd bear a son a year from then Sarah laughed to herself saying, "*After I am worn out, **and** my lord is old, shall I have pleasure?*" (v.12) Abraham's body was just as unable to take part in creating a child as Sarah's at their age, but yet he believed against the circumstances. He believed what God *said*, not what his body demonstrated to be true. So it was actually two individuals' bodies that were touched by the power of God to make this miracle happen. With that said faith *changes* circumstances.

Oh, and it says in Genesis 25:1-2 that after Sarah died, Abraham took another wife, whose name was Keturah, and it names six more kids Abraham had in that later marriage of which Scripture doesn't feel the need to give us more information about. But if you read between the lines, it looks to me like God over-healed Abraham, didn't He?! God didn't just provide enough healing virtue into Abraham and Sarah's bodies to finally create that spark of life that grew up to become Isaac. Pardon my euphemism, but God didn't turn the tap back off when He was done. Abraham had six more kids in his second century of life with his second wife. At any rate, God *over* provided for the need, even if it seemed like a long time coming on the front end of it, in hindsight it looks like God over did it for Abraham.

Do you *weaken in faith* (v.19)? Or do circumstances make you change your mind? Do you look at your body and say *"sorry God, it just won't happen."* Or do you look at your body and say, *"sorry body, but God said it will happen!"* Do you have expectation that things will change?

Some of these truths are life-changing and I know there are pessimistic Christians content to stay in the ruts they are in, but if you really want to rise above circumstances then I encourage you to meditate on this passage and ones like it and really absorb the principles in it.

Get to a point where your life resembles who this passage says Abraham was.

FAITH IS NOT MENTAL

As I mentioned a moment ago, faith is not merely mental assent about something. Let's camp out for a moment in a passage from the book of Hebrews:

> **By faith** Abraham **obeyed** when he was called to go out to a place that he was to receive as an inheritance. And he went out, **not knowing where he was going**.
> **By faith** he went to live in the land of promise, as in a foreign land, living in tents with Isaac and Jacob, heirs with him of the same promise.
> For he was looking forward to the city that has

> foundations, whose designer and builder is God.
>
> **By faith Sarah herself received power to conceive, even when she was past the age, since she considered him faithful who had promised.**
>
> Therefore from one man, and **him as good as dead**, were born descendants as many as the stars of heaven and as many as the innumerable grains of sand by the seashore.
>
> (*Heb 11:8-12, emphasis mine*)

Please, go back and re-read that passage again before moving forward. Did you do it? OK, I trust you. Let's proceed.

That whole chapter of the book of Hebrews is one worthy of study since we generally know it as the "hall of faith chapter", but that term gets thrown around so much we forget that it is the *faith* chapter.

The main thing that jumps out at me from looking at it is that *faith requires obedience*. Abraham didn't take time to think about it. He didn't go consult all his spiritual mentors to get a consensus on what he should do. The original passage in

Genesis tells us that when God called him, Abraham left his land. But not only that, he left not knowing where he was going.

If you're like me, you have to admit to yourself that everything in us fights this act of obedience, and we don't like stepping out UNLESS we know where God is taking us.

In my experience, whenever I've begun speaking a prophetic word for someone, I have no clue where I am going with it until I start to share the little God has already given me to say. I open my mouth, and share the little bit I know to share, and as I do, more enters into my spirit or comes to my mind to speak, and then more. Like a chain-link it just keeps coming and when I am done, I usually can't help but think, *"Man! I'm glad I stepped out and delivered that!"* But when prophesying, often you don't even have the whole message until you step out and begin to share that first "link" in the chain, and then the rest of the chain starts to come out as well.

Sometimes we mentally *know* that God heals and we give mental assent to the Scriptures, but we don't actually step out and pray for a sick person. The obedience required from faith would have us go for it and "not know where we're going" sometimes. I've had instances where I prayed for someone with one eye open in case what I was praying for really came to pass. I have to admit I had thoughts running through my mind like, "what am I doing!" and I didn't want to miss it. There's nothing wrong with *mentally* doubting things, but there's something wrong with not obeying God with the thing He's compelling you to step out and do.

Sometimes a doubtful thought goes into our head and we assume that because we have doubted, we have sinned, even if that doubtful thought came and went in just a split second. We think that because of that doubtful thought, we have sinned and have failed to act out or pray in faith. As a result of this moment of doubt, we think we will be punished and our prayers will not be answered.

I will never forget something from the climax from the 1980s movie *Ghostbusters*. Many of my generation saw this movie in their childhood so if you're too young to remember the movie, let me set up what I'm talking about. There's this woman-man-dude-monster-thing that the four main Ghostbusters have set out to annihilate. This androgynous being tells them they will be destroyed by whatever they imagine. Suddenly, out of nowhere comes this big giant King Kong-sized "Stay-puft Marshmallow Man" walking through the streets of New York City. Three of the characters look to a fourth one, played by Dan Aykroyd, as he explains that he tried to think of the most harmless thing possible, and the marshmallow man was what "just popped in" to his mind from his childhood. This was the way they were going to be destroyed — all because Dan Aykroyd's character let this thought enter into his mind.

Doubt is *not* like that, my friends.

Doubt is not accidentally having a thought pop into your mind saying *"this won't happen."* Real doubt and unbelief comes when, like the opposite of *obeying* in faith, you act on the doubt and don't step out in obedience. Doubt is when your belief that *"they won't get healed, therefore I won't bother trying"* becomes something you act on. Doubt and disobedience are tightly intertwined.

We don't know if Abraham, while packing up his stuff, had thoughts like, *"what if this God is a liar and He's not taking me anywhere?".* If he did, Abraham didn't act on these thoughts. I guarantee you if Abraham packed up his stuff and ideas were going through his head like, *"what if this is some kind of joke"*, from reading the account in Genesis we can see that clearly he didn't *act* on those doubts. If he truly doubted, he never would have left his homeland.

I know some of you are thinking of the passage in the first chapter of James that says, *"let him ask in faith without doubting,"* and about the double-minded man tossed by every wave, and so forth. Keep in mind what we've just established — that faith requires obedience or it is not really faith.

Faith Requires Obedience

For some reason I've never heard the following passage of Scripture used for any purpose other than legalism and salvation — people quoting from it to show how you're not a Christian because you *do* things, but doing things are fruit that you are saved, like how an apple tree grows apples and so on. While that is true and I have no problem with people using that passage to teach such, it goes further than that and a lot of practical application can be drawn from James 2:14-26. Give the following passage a careful read.

> What good is it, my brothers, if someone says he has faith but does not have works? **Can that faith save him?** If a brother or sister is poorly clothed and lacking in daily food, and one of you says to them, "Go in peace, be warmed and filled," without giving them the things needed for the body, what good is that? **So also faith by itself, if it does not have works, is dead.**
> But someone will say, "You have faith and I have works." **Show me your faith apart from your works, and I will show you my faith by my works.**

You believe that God is one; you do well. Even the demons believe–and shudder! Do you want to be shown, you foolish person, that **faith apart from works is useless**? Was not Abraham our father justified by works when he offered up his son Isaac on the altar? **You see that faith was active along with his works, and faith was completed by his works;** and the Scripture was fulfilled that says, "Abraham believed God, and it was counted to him as righteousness"–and he was called a friend of God. **You see that a person is justified by works and not by faith alone**. And in the same way was not also Rahab the prostitute justified by works when she received the messengers and sent them out by another way? **For as the body apart from the spirit is dead, so also faith apart from works is dead.** (*Emphasis mine*)

Remember how we've already established that faith is not mentally believing a chair will hold your weight IF you sit down on it. Faith is only faith when it is accompanied by the action of going ahead and sitting down in it and not worrying if the chair will cave in under you or not — even if you might be praying that the chair won't collapse under your weight! OK I'll stop meddling with you about your weight now. You know the chair won't give way, even though you may not have tried it sitting in that particular chair previously, and you may be totally unaware of whether all the legs are holding up properly or if there's anything else wrong with it not visible to the eye. You have no *evidence* yet that it will support your weight, other than for lack of a better word — *assuming* it will.

Abraham did not have faith just because mentally he believed God would keep His promise. His faith was demonstrated by how he left his home and followed God somewhere else. He had faith *because he demonstrated* it by putting Isaac on that altar (see Genesis chapter 22).

Faith has everything to do with action. Most people don't like that idea, but we can't sidestep that verse 26 says *"For as the body apart from the spirit is dead, so also faith apart from works is dead."*

It's not merely believing that God *can* speak words of knowledge about people to you for you to speak towards their edification — it's opening your mouth and sharing those words fully knowing and trusting God that you're speaking forth His heart and not your own imagination.

Faith is not merely believing that God *can* or *does* heal today. It's stepping out and receiving our own healing or laying hands on a sick person and they get better.

Faith is not merely believing *that* the Gospel is true, but as Romans 9 says it's believing in your heart *and doing* something — in this verse, it's *speaking* with your mouth that Jesus is Lord — which by the way is *not just* a salvation prayer (if it is even that), but is a constant and continual lifestyle, not just a one time thing.

For example, Romans says in the tenth chapter,

> *"if you confess with your mouth that Jesus is Lord and believe in your heart that God raised him from the dead, you will be saved. For with the heart one believes and is justified, and with the mouth one confesses and is saved." (v. 9-10)*

In this case, the accompanying action is saying something. Speaking. It's a confession, a declaration that you believe Jesus Christ died on the cross and purchased your salvation from sin with his blood.

There are many things about faith that are not simply believing in your heart, but faith constitutes appropriate actions or declarations that accompany these beliefs. Sometimes I encounter people who say to me, "*I agree (or believe) with you Steve that the Bible says this or that."* They say this about any particular topic, but especially a topic related to miracles or healing. In my mind I can't help but think to myself, *"well so what if you believe that? — I don't see how you're **living** like it — there's no demonstration accompanying your confession."* The same can be true with people who say to me they are Christians but are in actuality living a lifestyle of sin and immorality, or they simply exhibit the fruit *opposite* of what the Bible says is fruit of the Holy Spirit. OK, *these* people I *do* say something to them! It doesn't matter if you say you *mentally* agree with it if you don't demonstrate fruit worthy of repentance. It requires almost nothing of us to mentally believe something is true or accurate. The rubber meets the road when we *act* on the truth.

What does the Word of God say our Master will tell His servants on that day? *"Well believed my good and faithful servant?"* No but well *done*. I repeat myself, but I'm not saying actions are what make us right with God — that's legalism. Accepting Jesus Christ's finished work on the cross and letting the fruit be produced in our lives, resulting in actions demonstrating our faith, this demonstrates we belong to God and that we are obeying what the Lord says in His Word.

Would Rahab the prostitute be recorded as an example in James here if she only "believed in her heart" that the two spies were from Israel and that God was giving Israel the land of Canaan? If she merely believed, she and her family would not have been spared. It was by her actions that Scripture records her actions and honors her so many generations later for us to read about.

In conclusion, I repeat it again: faith involves action, not just mere thoughts.

FAITH FOR THE IMPOSSIBLE

Before proceeding further, let me establish that it's NOT true that all believers have an "equal amount" of faith. Or at least let me qualify that. Yes, God gives each of us the same "seed" if you will. Baby Christians for example would have a hard time believing God, or you His servant, if you spoke to them something on His behalf. Such as if you told them grand supernatural things that God was going to do using them. On the other hand someone who's older and more mature in the Lord should have been stretched and gone through enough experiences in life that he could see for himself in his own life how God's promises are yes and amen in Him (2 Cor 2:20).

Each of us begins at the point we've accepted Jesus Christ as our personal savior — the moment of the new birth with an equal measure of faith. From this point onward the believer is shaped by experiences and how much of the Word of God they choose to eat. They can eat it in bites, or they can devour it. Individuals can have the faith to be saved and be converted at the same point in time, and some will outpace others by leaps and bounds as to the depths in God they choose to go into. Unfortunately, others still drag their feet and never leave their diapers behind even into adulthood.

What is the simplest and most obvious way to increase your faith? Trials and tests. Great faith comes by great tests. It doesn't come just by feeding on God's Word. Nor does it come from listening to great preaching podcasts or mp3s, or reading a lot of books by faith teachers. The potential for great faith comes by hearing the Word of Christ (Romans 10:17).

Great faith comes when you put what you've heard into practice. Athletes don't build muscle by knowing how to. They get stronger from actually building muscles. How do they do it? They work out in the gym. They go for runs or make sure they eat healthily. But with exercise they use their muscles against something. No pain, no gain. They don't get bulked up and physically fit from just reading books about how to exercise — they actually exercise! To build faith muscle, you have to use your faith against something. You need some kind of pressure put on you, whether it be from the Heavenly Father allowing us to be tested, or whether it be our reaction to demonic attack over our lives through finances, health, or other various and typical circumstances the enemy attacks us through.

Miraculous formation of an unborn baby's brain

I once heard a second-hand account of a man who found out that his unborn daughter was going to be born with only a quarter of her normal brain fully formed. In response to this, the man quit his job and got all the healing and faith preachings he could get his hands on. All day he would listen to these preachings while he paced the floor of his living room, as if it were a full time job. Then, after a few weeks, when he was convinced in his spirit of God's will for his daughter to be born whole and not lacking, he found all the Scriptures in the Word of God dealing with the subject and would pace his living room floor while praying in the Holy Spirit and confessing these verses out loud. He would read simple Bible verses that were just "typical" healing passages and quote them out loud for hours. Then after about 5 or 6 hours had passed, he would just thank God for the miracle He had already provided as if it had already came to pass. He knew what 1 John 5:14-15 said concerning believing that we've received. Then he'd go to bed and start the same routine again the next day.

You're likely reading that and thinking *"that's insane!"*, but that's what this man decided was necessary to bring himself to a place where he could confidently expect God to move in his daughter's body. He didn't do this stuff to "get God to heal" her, but to bring *himself* to a place of faith where he could believe he received what God already gave. That part right there, that God already provides things and it's up to us to obtain them by faith confounds many people who believe that in God's sovereignty He picks some to die prematurely for some higher purpose. Wrong! God doesn't kill babies because He "needs another flower in His garden".

Needless to say, the man and his wife continued to get ultrasounds done by their doctor, and each time they saw that the baby's brain had grown bigger and bigger until eventually it was fully formed. She was born totally and fully functional, and at the time of the article that I heard this from, the child was 5 or 6 years old and had no unusual health problems in her life to that point. This man did what it took to bring himself to a place of faith to obtain the promise.

Many people don't want to persevere to obtain their miracle because many believe if you don't get the answer right away then that means God's answer is "no" and it's improper to keep persisting (I'll just recommend my book *6 Lies People Believe About Divine Healing* again to tackle that lie in more detail than I will here). I often wonder if these same people have read the parable of the persistent widow in Luke 11.

Personal Testimonies

Back in the spring and summer of 2005, I was doing a six-month internship in Leeuwarden, The Netherlands. I had saved up a decent amount of money over the previous winter from working and fundraising and had enough money to last me my entire internship. In August of that year we did a two week summer school, which is similar to a retreat or conference, only it lasts for two weeks. Guest speakers were flown in from the United States, and we had class sessions three times per day, along with our meals and dormitories for sleeping. I had not been made aware of the extra expense of 300 euros that I needed to come up with to pay my part, in order to participate in the school. I honestly can't remember how God came through with the money, even though He did, so that's not the focus of the testimony I'm about to share.

Two days after the summer school ended, there was an opportunity for me to go to Italy for six days and join a missions team from my Bible school in North Carolina. My mentor and friend, John Cava was leading the group, and at age 24, I wanted to take advantage of any and every opportunity to travel to other places in Europe if at all possible during my internship -- especially if they were for ministry opportunities. Ironically enough, while I was in Bible school I never once went on a mission trip. I simply never had the money and with the issues surrounding my visa to attend the school as an international student (since you know, Canada is NOT a part of the United States), I was afraid of having difficulty getting back into the USA if I ever went abroad during school breaks.

So while in the FIRE Holland summer school I had booked a flight one night at a nearby restaurant that permitted us to use their WiFi internet service. Immediately after booking my flight, two different friends gave me money for the trip without me having to ask publicly or let anybody know I had any need. One friend gave me 100 euros, and the other 75 euros, which basically covered my round trip flight from Amsterdam to Rome.

There was a daily cost for room and board, just like at the summer school in Holland, and in no time I spent all the money I had left. I began to doubt if I was really supposed to have gone on that trip. Was it God's will or did I act in presumption and waste my money?

I came back home to Leeuwarden the next week on either a Monday or Tuesday, and shared with my housemates, who were missionaries, about the street outreaches I got to participate in and how I got to pray with many young men to receive the baptism in the Holy Spirit who then spoke in tongues for the first time in their lives. I also shared of how I got to have a great time fellowshipping with others who had gone on that trip. In fact, to this day I'm still in regular contact with some of the Italian brothers I met on that trip thanks to social media like Facebook. My housemates encouraged me that this was not a waste of time and that God knew my needs and He would come through.

That Wednesday night when we had our weekly house church meeting, I shared what God had done on that trip. If I mentioned any need to them that night, I don't remember it. On this particular occasion there were guests whom I had never seen before: a young twenty-something African woman and an older lady, who turned out to be her mother. I did not know either of their names, but they had come on the recommendation of their pastor, who was a friend of ours. We fellowshipped, worshipped Jesus, and someone shared a teaching like usual. Afterwards we drank tea and ate stroopwaffels — a Dutch treat *you have got to try* if you ever visit the Netherlands!

Before our two visitors left, the younger woman gave me an envelope and said it was from her mom — the other woman who was present with her that night but who seemed to have already left and was waiting outside. I could tell from touching it that it clearly had some currency in the envelope. I thanked her sincerely and maybe too profusely because without even knowing the quantity, I was already elated that God was coming through for me.

As soon as she left, I walked to another room briefly out of sight, and opened the envelope to see how much money was in it. I was shocked — it contained 460 euros! In those days, with the exchange rate at that time, it was close to $600 USD. I immediately showed it to a few members of my team, and everybody praised God with me that He had provided. The amount in the envelope was almost double what I needed.

God provided more than I spent. He provided and then some. This messed with my head at the time when I used to believe God would only provide for things I *needed*, and not things I desire or I may have been suffering consequences for due to my own presumption.

It should be mentioned that I have never been comfortable sharing publicly when I've lacked or needed financial breakthrough. So in the following testimony a couple of years later, I didn't let anybody know the need for finances I found myself in one time when I was now living in Holland.

In the beginning of 2007, I returned to the Netherlands as a missionary after spending a few months in Canada itinerating. During my first two months back in the country, I received none of the financial support I had been counting on and thought I had raised while back home. My parents sent me some money, but *Calvary International Canada*, my Canadian missions covering, e-mailed me explaining the reason no money was deposited into my bank account was because no money had come in for me. Yikes! I have been in very tight spots before, but this was tighter than usual.

Much of the previous 6 years of my life to that point I'd lived in other countries unable to legally work in them. I had to believe God for my jar to not run empty, but it overflowed only by His miraculous provision. Since I was already in the habit of praying for extended periods in tongues in the basement at our team's *Firehouse* café in afternoons or evenings when we were closed, I started to find Scriptures that talked about God meeting my needs and passages about money. I would write out Scripture memory cards and pace the floor of the café and read them over and over again out loud, confessing the Word over my problems like I'm encouraging you to do in your situation.

I did not *ask* God for money — I thanked Him for *already providing* it. I thanked Him for the various ways and methods He had decided to get it to me that I did not know about yet. Harold Collins, the director at CIC at the time used to say God told us to pray for our *daily* bread, not our *monthly* bread. I'm still finding that true! I still never lacked, and I ate nicely, and had no overdue bills.

Immediately after discovering this "crisis", I found out that my American agency at that time, *F.I.R.E. International*, had deposited almost $400 US into my account! Since most of my support came through Canada, I hadn't checked my American account in days. What did come in through F.I. would usually only cover my expenses with them producing my newsletters and mailing them to Canada for me, and diverting small amounts toward other missionaries I wanted to sow into.

When I discovered this amount was in there I immediately withdrew it and lived off of it for how long it lasted. Not only that, but a month later I saw my support spike up to a level higher than what's normally "pledged" to be there every month. I could go into detail of other things, like having Dutch friends paying for things for me or blessing me monetarily. The fact of the matter is that in the natural realm I could not have foreseen that happening while pacing the *Firehouse* floor in prayer during that whole winter season. Not with my natural eyes, anyway.

It usually takes pressure or a crisis before we find out what kind of faith we have, and many Christians are more sheltered from that than they realize. Sudden calamity is the only way many of us are confronted with the opportunity to put our faith into practice. This is an effective way to grow in our faith and probably yields the most lasting results, but there are other ways. As Smith Wigglesworth said, great victories come out of great battles.

You and I are in charge of how we're going to respond in the face of crisis — does God really mean what He said in His Word, or not? How we respond to God in these situations determines how our faith will develop.

One more testimony and we'll move on. My wife Lili and I met through the missional community we are both part of in a place called Chorrillos, just outside of the nation of Peru's capital of Lima. She lived with our leaders for several years and naturally we formed a friendship when I joined their team. Within months of moving here we began dating, sensing it was the Lord's will for our lives, and in May of 2013 we were married.

After several months we decided to plan for a three or four week trip to Canada in the summer of 2012, as I would typically return home for a minimum of four to six weeks each year to visit family and churches that are supporting me on the mission field. This time, I had to believe God for double the amount since I would be taking Lili with me. So, I invested some money in two suitcases full of Alpaca products to sell to my Canadian friends to help offset the cost, and in early August off to Canada we went, hoping to sell the alpaca scarves and winter hats we had brought with us.

A few days before we were scheduled to return back to Peru, I had an email from a man I used to do a lot of freelance work for. He had been paying me to write a lot of content on his website and other things that had helped finance me on the mission field that year. He had gone broke and was contemplating shutting down the digital magazine he had started. In so many words, he was kindly warning me that he would no longer be able to afford paying me for an unforeseen amount of time. This was difficult news to hear because the work I did for him was more than enough to pay my monthly rent. Now Lili and I were faced with a decision — either we return to Peru and figure out another way to make up that income or support, or stay longer in Canada and raise more support. We checked our tickets and this was going to cost us another $500 each to stay one more month — which we weren't even sure was a long enough amount of time to stay and itinerate.

After praying about it, we were certain we needed to stay one month longer for the month of September and return to Peru after that. But we still had no idea how to afford the tickets without borrowing money from someone.

We were originally scheduled to return on September the 3rd, which was Labor Day Monday in North America. Lili and I were sitting on my parent's living room couch upstairs while they were watching TV in the basement. We were praying together and talking about options and possibilities when the phone rang. It was a friend of mine who was calling under the impression it was the last time he'd see us before we flew back to Peru the following Monday. He was inviting us to come over and spend some time praying together, something we had done several times before, while seeking the presence of God and prophesying over each other. I didn't hesitate to tell him that we'd love to, and that we were in a situation of significant need for finances. I hung up the phone after telling him we'd be there in 15 minutes.

I then repeated to Lili the gist of the conversation as I logged onto the internet to charge the tickets to my credit card. As a general rule, I don't use credit or borrow money, spending only within my means, but under the circumstances I felt we had no other choice. As I was getting ready to book the tickets, the phone rang. It was this brother again. He told me that he thought about what I said on the phone a moment ago and proceeded to tell me that he had $2000 CAD in the bank and wanted to loan it to me. I resisted at first and kept telling him, "thank you, but no." I knew he didn't have much of an income, and even if he had this amount of money to give me, the last thing I'd wanted to come between us in our friendship is that kind of money. I can think of no other prayer warrior who spends as much time praying for me as he does, and I had no idea if and when I'd ever be able to pay him back.

Nevertheless, we went to his house and prayed together and we all decided to sleep on the decision. We wanted to make absolutely sure he felt like giving this blessing to us the next day, without any reservations. The next day when we visited him to follow up on his offer, he insisted all was well and we drove him to his bank to withdraw the money, and then we went to my bank to deposit the cash into my account quickly before anybody could rob us if they saw we had that much cash on hand!

This unforeseen blessing was a very direct and literal answer to prayer. God came though and gave us the ability to afford our tickets, plus extra money to spend on gas as we travelled to a few different places around central Ontario that month. In the weeks to come, the brother who gave me this loan told me God had spoken to him to forgive the loan and turn it into a straightforward gift. I was stunned, but not really too surprised the more I thought about it afterward and contemplated how good God has been in his faithfulness and his provision.

If God has told you to do something, He will provide for it. If you are in need, God is concerned and hears your prayers.

Months later, while I was back in Peru this brother went to visit my parents in order to contact me over Skype since he doesn't have internet in his home. He told me that through some kind of mix up, the provincial government of Ontario realized they owed him back pay for some kind of assistance he receives from them for a medical condition he has. Can you guess at this point what the amount of back pay was? You guessed right if you said $2,000 CAD! Stepping out in faith and giving the amount he had saved to a missionary was something God rewarded him for and gave right back to him.

At this point you may be concerned that all my personal testimonies are related to money. *"Oh no, a prosperity name it and claim it book!"* That's not true. However, in my experience, the majority of the times I've been in desperate situations and seeking God or having my faith stretched have usually been related to money. If you think about it, one of the most important things we need in our natural lives is provision, for without it we can't buy food, we could not pay our rent or pay our other bills. It's very likely that you purchased this book and as you think of the situations in your life, you too need a financial breakthrough more than any other type of miracle. This book is not a book specifically about financial miracles, but everything taught in this book will apply to having faith for finances just much as having faith for a healing in your body or a loved one to come to Christ through your intercession. The instructions and advice in this book are all scalable — meaning, the prayer of faith will work whether you need something big or small — the principles are still the same!

Did you know there's only one recorded instance in all of the Gospels where the disciples asked Jesus to increase their faith? If you take a red-letter Bible and turn to Luke's Gospel account, you'll notice that Jesus shared several teachings and parables in succession from the fifteenth chapter onward with a common thread throughout all of them, money. The parable of the lost coin (money) with the woman finding it and celebrating (v. 8-10), followed by the parable of the prodigal son — who wasted his inheritance (money) and came back to his father's house. The sixteenth chapter then begins with the story of unrighteous steward who cancels many peoples' debts (of money) that they owed his master (1-13), followed by the parable of the rich man and Lazarus in the second half of the chapter. The rich man had everything in this life while the poor man who begged at his gate inherited "everything" in eternity. It is then after hearing all these teaching parables that Jesus talks about how it would be much better to tie a rock around one's neck and throw themselves in the sea than to offend a little one. It seems to be in regards to the points raised in his previous parables, and the importance of forgiving those we have offenses with regarding this issue.

Jesus undoubtedly is using these teachings to make a more profound point about forgiveness and salvation, but by using every day language and subject matter his audience were familiar with — such as money. After this particular series of parables, mostly concerning offense over money in some fashion, the disciples ask in Luke 17:5 for Jesus to increase their faith. For what it's worth, without going off on an unintended tangent I believe this had to do with asking for faith not to let money be an issue or an offense in their lives.

Later on in this book we'll examine Mark's account of speaking to mountains and casting them into the sea. Suffice it to say, there's little wrong with increasing your faith for finances since Scripture has a lot to say on the matter. Let's continue talking about some practical ways to increase our faith and remain in peace for God's provision.

A simple way to increase your faith: practice

Ask God for something small or trivial, like a new pair of socks — especially if you are NOT going to go out and buy them yourself. Find some simple thing you need and can't afford or can't accomplish on your own, and put your faith into the promises of God's willingness to provide for you. A pair of socks is simple enough. Pray about it and believe for the provision. Pick a specific color. If someone gives you a pair of white socks and you've been praying and believing for black socks, then thank God that He gave you the white socks, but keep believing for the ones you asked for. Most people make the mistake of believing "good enough" is God's best. No, it just means that while waiting to give you the black socks you've been asking for, He decided to give you a pair of white socks as well, and the other ones are still on the way.

You probably think I'm being ridiculous, and I am but for a reason. Despise not the day of small beginnings, and if your faith needs to grow, then start with things you can "almost" handle. People don't go from obtaining the socks they ask for in prayer to moving mountains and splattering grandma's goiter all over the wall by faith through prayer overnight, do they?

Feel free to email me at fireonyourhead@stevebremner.com and let me know if you got that pair of socks you were believing for. Or email me to share any other testimony of believing for something by faith that you were inspired to do. I'd love to hear it and be encouraged!

WHY STUDY FAITH?

The Bible is clear about what promises we are to obtain by faith, and what faith produces in our lives or what lack of it will fail to produce. If God places within our hands the means whereby faith can be produced or manifested, then the responsibility of whether we act on it or not rests upon us. It is therefore necessary to know how this takes place if we are planning on going further into the promises of God that we obtain by faith.

> Romans 12:3: *"For by the grace of God given to me, I say to everyone among you not to think of himself more than he ought to think, but to think with sober judgment, each according to* **the measure of faith God has assigned.**"

We are each given a measure or amount of faith, by the grace of God.

> Ephesians 2:8: *"For by grace you have been saved through faith. And this is not your own doing; it is the **gift of God**."*

The measure of faith that we have each received is a gift from God, and He has given it based on His grace towards us. We don't *earn* faith, it is a gift given.

> Romans 10:17: "So **faith comes from hearing**, *and hearing through the Word of Christ."*

This verse is relatively simple and straightforward: Hearing the Word of God produces faith. Therefore, it's a good idea to make sure to read and study the Word of God, speak it and meditate on it, just like the following verse says:

> 2 Cor. 4:13: *"Since we have the same spirit of faith according to what has been written "I **believed**, and so I **spoke**," we also **believe**, and so we also **speak**."*

What we believe influences what we speak. The Bible also says out of the abundance of the heart the mouth speaks (Matt 12:34). What is in your heart? What are you saying?

> 2 Thess. 1:3: *"We ought to always give thanks to God for you, brothers, as is right, because your **faith is growing** abundantly, and the love of every one of you for one another is increasing."*

According to this Scripture, our faith can grow. If it can grow abundantly, then the opposite must also be possible, in that believers can fail to grow in the area of faith. If it can grow or stay small, then that must mean believers can be at different degrees of growth when it comes to having faith, would it not? Therefore, it's possible, and necessary to increase (grow) your faith.

> Romans 4:19-20: *"He did not weaken in faith when he considered his own body, which was as good as dead (since he was a hundred years old), or when he considered the barrenness of Sarah's womb. No distrust made him waver concerning the promise of God, but he **grew strong in his faith** as he gave glory to God."*

We can be strong in faith, or we can be weak in faith. Notice Abraham grew strong in his faith as he gave glory to God. It's reasonable to assume that your faith will grow if you decide to glorify God while you're waiting for the promise you are believing for to finally come to pass. Don't keep asking God to fulfill His promise, but glorify Him and thank Him for it.

> 1 John 5:14-15 says *"And this is the confidence we have toward Him, that if we ask anything according to His will, he hears us. And **if we know that He hears us in whatever we ask**, we know that we have the requests that we have asked of Him."*

Thank God and praise Him for the answer to your prayer before the answer has been manifested. This is KEY to seeing the promise fulfilled.

> Philippians 4:6-7 also brings this to light, as it says *"Do not be anxious about anything, but in everything by prayer and supplication with thanksgiving let your requests be made known to God. And the peace of God, which surpasses all understanding, will guard your hearts and your minds in Christ Jesus."*

If we believe God has granted us the answer to what we ask of Him, we will not be anxious in waiting for its fulfillment. Anxiety over if God will fulfill His promise is symptomatic of a heart that is uncertain of whether God will in fact answer. If you are seeking something He has promised in His Word, then you can know His will on the matter and seek the answer more confidently. If you don't give your prayer with supplication AND thanksgiving (before the answer has come) then God won't, in turn, guard your heart and give you the peace that keeps you from being anxious about it.

Another important component to developing faith is found in Hebrews 11. The whole chapter is great, but for brevity's sake, let's look at verse 6 which says,

> "And **without faith it is impossible to please Him**, for whoever would draw near to God must believe that He is and that He rewards those who seek Him."

If you have a translation of the Bible that phrases it to say that believers are to believe that God "exists", then grab a pen and scribble the word out and write "is" instead. Many modern translations mistranslate this when the original text has a connotation of God "being" [as He is]. Believers in Jesus Christ ALREADY know that He exists! What are believers to believe God "is"? As the rest of the verse says — that He is a rewarder of those who seek Him.

The believer will have a hard time standing on any promise in the Word of God if they stumble over the fact that God is the provider or any other character trait made clear in His word about Himself. "God is not a man, that he should lie, nor a son of man, that he should change his mind. Does he speak and then not act? Does he promise and not fulfill?" (Num 23:19) Any doubt of whom God is and if He will perform what He has promised will cause the believer not to seek Him Who is a rewarder of those who seek Him. It's as simple as that.

> *Truly, I say to you, whoever says to this mountain, 'Be taken up and thrown into the sea,' and does not doubt in his heart, but believes that what he says will come to pass, it will be done for him. Therefore I tell you, whatever you ask in prayer,* **believe that you have received it, and it will be yours**. (Mark 11:23-24)

Jesus never told us only to believe. But He did tell us to speak and believe that we will have the things we say. This can sound too much like "name it and claim it, blab it and grab it" and be off putting to some believers. However, we can't ignore the relationship between speaking and what we believe. What are we told in this passage to believe? That the things we say will come to pass. So, what are you saying? Are you whining all the time about your problems? Or are you speaking victory and freedom? We are told to speak to the mountain what God's Word says, but most Christians speak to God about the mountain.

Too many Christians are like Pharisees and don't have any clue that they are. I'm not talking about legalistic obedience of man-made rules — I'm talking of the ones who won't and don't believe until they see. That's not faith. Faith is being sure of what we hope for and certain of what we do not see (Hebrews 11:1). If you could see it, then that wouldn't be faith. When most Christians say they're cautious and skeptical of something (like healing) and they won't accept it until they see it for themselves, they're really just broadcasting their ignorance and unbelief. Believing it when you see it is knowledge, not faith. These believers are walking by sight, not faith. Bless their hearts.

More Scripture verses to increase your faith

> James 2:5: *"Listen, my beloved brothers, has not God chosen those who are poor in the world to be **rich in faith** and heirs of the kingdom, which He has promised to those who love Him?"*

If we can be rich in faith, we can be poor in faith also, wouldn't you agree? It doesn't take being poor in this world's standards to be rich in faith either, you know!

> Acts 6:5a: *"And what they said pleased the whole gathering, and they chose Stephen, a man **full of faith** and the Holy Spirit"*

If we can be full of faith, do you think we can be empty and lacking it? Or running on near empty?

> James 2:22: *"You see that **faith was active** along with his works, and faith was completed by his works."*

Again, I hope my over-simplification of these verses doesn't sound condescending or patronizing, but many Christians don't think of these things: if your faith can be active, it can be inactive. It can lack actions to demonstrate or go along with the confession of your mouth. Faith is active and demonstrated by actions, not just a mental belief.

> 1 Tim 1:5: *"The aim of our charge is love that issues from a pure heart and a good conscience and a **sincere faith**."*

If faith can be sincere, it can be insincere.

> 1 Tim 1:19: *"**Holding faith** and a good conscience. By rejecting this some have made **shipwreck of their faith**."*

How do people shipwreck their faith, by the way?

> 1 John 5:4: *"For everyone who has been born of God overcomes the world. And this is the victory that has overcome the world – our faith."*

Faith is how we overcome. If we are not overcoming, is it possible, according to this verse that maybe–just maybe–we aren't walking in our faith? If our faith is how we overcome, then yes!

I strongly suggest going over all these verses for yourself, memorizing them, studying them, and familiarizing yourself with them even if you think you already know them. I admit I don't like formulas, but the following is something that can help you if you're facing a mountain you need to speak to and throw into the sea. When you do, make sure you have your bathing suit on too as we'll look at more below.

1. Find a promise in God's Word for whatever you are seeking.
2. Believe God's word as you would the word from a friend.
3. Do not consider the contradictory circumstances
4. Praise God for the answer, acting on the Word of God.

BELIEVE THAT YOU HAVE RECEIVED IT

*"Therefore I tell you, whatever you ask in prayer, **believe that you have received it**, and it will be yours."* (Mark 11:24, emphasis mine)

Every so often I am told by people that I'm a "faith teacher" in a derogatory way as if studying about, living this out, and writing about faith is a bad thing. Sometimes people rightly perceive this to be one of my favorite topics, or that I'm not capable of writing or preaching about any other subject. I assume this is because of the frequency with which I constantly remind people to "believe they have already received it", which is Biblical.

I'm hardly ever offended by such notions since the Word of God says "the just shall live by faith" (Hab 2:4, Rom 1:17, Gal

3:11, Heb 10:38) and Hebrews 11:6 says *"without faith it is impossible to please him: for he that cometh to God must believe that He is, and that he is a rewarder of them that diligently seek Him."* (King James Version) Therefore, I don't understand how one could allegedly spend too much time finding out how to live like a righteous person in God's eyes, and how to please Him in the Christian walk!

The key thing about faith to remember is that it is always based on the promise already stated. This is what distinguishes it from hope. Hope doesn't know for certain what will or could happen, but it longs for the desired result. Faith however, stands on some kind of prior knowledge, what has already been established–the assurance of things hoped for, the conviction of things not seen (see Hebrews 11:1). The believer needs to stick to the Word of God, and have confidence based on what is written in Scripture, and like the context of this particular verse states, then you will know what to speak to the mountainous problem you may be facing.

Therefore, another key to increasing your faith is changing your focus. Instead of focusing on the problem don't just speak to it, but find out what exactly the Word of God already says about that situation or circumstance, and how a believer is to face it. Then focus on that and only speak of the victory Christ promised, and not give any voice to any discouragement tempting you.

Faith looks at something as if it is already done because it knows that it is and nothing shakes that. However, hope has no such specific assurance but flows out of faith–it can only hope for the desired outcome because it relies on what has been promised. Faith is the acceptance of God's fact–it has already happened, God already spoke it and promised and gave it through His Son. As a result, you now believe that you have already received it and you will see it.

Hope on the other hand trusts in something still future because of what it already knows and accepts as fact. Just because the Christian might still struggle with sin or be living in a lifestyle of sin doesn't contradict that he has (in the past tense) been purchased with the blood of Christ and is made a new creation. The way faith would be applied to this significant fact is to look at the word "reckon" — or as other translations like the English Standard Version tell us — "consider" as used in in the following context:

> *"For the death he died* (past tense) *he died to sin, once* (past tense) *for all, but the life he lives he lives to God. So you also must consider yourselves dead* (past tense) *to sin and alive to God in Christ Jesus. Let not sin therefore reign in your mortal body, to make you obey its passions."* (Romans 6:10-12 ESV, emphasis and parenthesis mine)

You cannot reckon or consider anything without first having had the concept or idea introduced to you to be able to ponder it or think of it and act on the knowledge you've been given. 'Reckon' or 'consider' are words that only relate to the past in this regard, and give context to the word 'therefore' which leads into what is to take place now in the present for the believer: not letting sin reign in your mortal body, based on the act that has happened–you have died to sin, because of what Christ has done.

The way to overcoming sin is to consider or reckon what the Word of God has already stated concerning what has already been accomplished at the Cross of Calvary by our Lord Jesus Christ. In this case He died and overcame sin, and that you who have given your life to Christ, were hidden in Him. By that, you died with Him when He hung on the cross. Therefore, you substantiate that into existence in your own life as a Christian. As Watchman Nee says in his book *The Normal Christian Life*,

> "All temptation is primarily to look within, to take our eyes off the Lord and to take account of appearances. Faith is always meeting a mountain, a mountain of evidence that seems to contradict God's Word, a mountain of apparent contradiction in the realm of tangible fact–of failures in deed, as well as in the realm of feelings and suggestion–and

either faith or the mountain has to go. They cannot both stand. But the trouble is that many a time the mountain stays and faith goes. That must not be. If we resort to our senses to discover the truth, we shall find Satan's lies are often enough true to our experience, but if we refuse to accept as binding anything that contradicts God's Word and maintain an attitude of faith in Him alone, we shall find instead that Satan's lies begin to dissolve and that our experience is coming progressively to tally with that Word." [1]

In other words, God gave you the gift of holiness -- you believe that you have already received it, and you will be holy. Amen for that!

By faith Abraham obeyed when he was called (past tense promise) *to go out to a place that he was to receive as an inheritance. And he went out not knowing where he was going... For he was looking forward to the city that has foundations, whose designer and builder is God.* (Heb 11:8, 10, parenthesis mine)

Despite the decades that passed before Abraham and Sarah would see the promise fulfilled and give birth to their son Isaac, they had the promise of the word of the Lord when He told him *"Look up at the heavens and count the stars — if indeed you can count them. So shall your offspring be."* (Gen 15:5)

They hung on to this promise given them in order to have the hope that it would be fulfilled.

> *"No distrust made him waver concerning the promise of God, but he grew strong in his faith as he gave glory to God, fully convinced that God was able to do what He had promised"* (Rom 4:20-21)
>
> *By faith Sarah herself received power to conceive, even when she was past the age, since she considered* (or reckoned) *him faithful who had promised.* (Heb 11:11, parenthesis mine).

Despite the dreams of leadership given to him years earlier in his youth, Joseph did not look like he'd be ruling anybody or anything while he was locked away in a dungeon. I have always imagined these dreams and the promises they meant would go through Joseph's mind many a night as he lay shackled in a dark dungeon forgotten by the very people he'd helped. He reckoned that God would do what He said He would with his life.

Or what of the promise the Lord made Moses concerning leading the people out of Egypt? It didn't look like it was about to come to pass when immediately after speaking to the

Pharaoh, their work quota was increased, and it took ten plagues before he finally had enough and released the Israelites to go on their way. I'm sure Moses reckoned that God would do what He said, and could cling to that promise despite the natural circumstances looking like they were getting more and more difficult.

Despite the prophecies about Jesus Christ, our example and Savior, it didn't appear to the Pharisees standing, watching, and mocking that He was going to save or rule anybody, let alone look like He'd live when He hung there bloody, naked, and twisted upon a wooden cross. Yet what was spoken would come to pass. Oftentimes the promise is the most difficult to believe in right before its eventual fulfillment. We could go on with many more examples from Scripture of people receiving that which they were promised, and if you read through Hebrews 11, you'll notice the same pattern written of a promise made followed by an expectation of fulfillment by most of the people mentioned there.

Also consider how Isaiah 55:11 says

> *"For as the rain and the snow come down from heaven and do not return there but water the earth, making it bring forth and sprout, giving seed to the sower and bread to the eater, so shall my word be that goes out from my mouth; it shall not return to*

> *me empty, but it shall accomplish that which I purpose, and shall succeed in the thing for which I sent it."*

God's written and spoken Word will be accomplished, since God is not a man that He can lie (Num 23:19), and if He has spoken it in the Bible, you can rely on it and put your confidence in the Lord about the matter. What He has already spoken, will come to pass. If He has spoken to you in the prayer closet you can rest assured He will perform what He said He would, for the very word He gave you often times was to give you an anchor to hang on to when the circumstances immediately following it test your confidence in the matter. So believe that you have received it. It is done. If you need healing in your body, then learn from these figures in the Bible who were put there as our example and take courage. Be like Abraham who did not consider (or reckon) in his old age that producing a child with his wife was impossible.

> *"Do not be anxious about anything, but in everything by prayer and supplication with thanksgiving let your requests be made known to God. And the peace of God, which surpasses all understanding, will guard your hearts and your minds in Christ Jesus."* (Phil 4:6-7)

There's power in our words, and it's important to be confessing the right things with our mouths. We will focus on the power of our confession in a later section.

1. Watchman Nee, *The Normal Christian Life*, (Fort Washington, Christian Literature Crusade) p 72.

IS MUSTARD SEED REALLY ENOUGH TO SPEAK TO THE MOUNTAINS IN YOUR LIFE?

Truly, I say to you, whoever says to this mountain, 'Be taken up and thrown into the sea,' and does not doubt in his heart, but believes that what he says will come to pass, it will be done for him. Therefore I tell you, whatever you ask in prayer, believe that you have received it, and it will be yours. (Mark 11:23-24)

And Jesus answered, "O faithless and twisted generation, how long am I to be with you? How long am I to bear with you? Bring him here to me." And Jesus rebuked the demon, and it came out of him, and the boy was healed instantly. Then the disciples came to Jesus privately and said, "Why could we not cast it out?" He said to them, "Because of your little faith. For truly, I say to you, if you have faith like a grain of mustard seed, you will say to this mountain, 'Move from here to there,'

> *and it will move, and nothing will be impossible for you."* (Matthew 17:17-20)

There's this erroneous sacred cow in many Christian circles that it's rude to teach people to have more faith than they already do. Many teach and preach that "all it takes is faith the size of a mustard seed to move mountains." Not so. If it took faith the size of a mustard seed, we'd have all the mountains moved already. The passage in Matthew's Gospel where Jesus makes the statement about one having faith like — not the *size* of — a grain of mustard seed and it can move a mountain immediately follows the incident where the disciples were unable to cast a demon out of a boy. He then told them they failed to do it because of their little faith. So likewise, this passage in Mark is NOT saying faith can be small and accomplish major things.

Notice that in Mark's Gospel account Jesus cursed the fig tree and then keeps going on his way to the temple which he cleanses. Then, according to verse 20, they passed by it the next morning and saw the results of the word Jesus spoke. He didn't lay a hand on it and proclaim a lightning bolt to zap it. He cursed it with His words. There's the power of life and death in the tongue, and we can use it for blessing or cursing (James 3:9-11). This is an example of it being used for righteously cursing something.

Sometimes people's main objection to faith for divine healing is lack of instantaneous results, but we need to remember something: the fig tree didn't demonstrate any outward evidence that it had been cursed and would no longer bear fruit. According to this account, it may not have been noticeable until a day later. Sometimes speaking the Word of God over our circumstances doesn't yield a noticeable result right away. However, in the Spirit the prayer has been answered and the outward circumstances are already in the process of changing. Maybe the cancer in someone's body has been removed, and now the body needs normal healing to recuperate from all the damage that the stupid curse has caused. We must remember that we walk by faith and not by sight, and sometimes appearances don't tell the whole story. Like the fig tree, the roots of a problem can be dealt with but the branches don't look dead right away.

That leads me to my next point. Do you really think you'll have the guts to speak to a mountain in your life if you only have a little bit of faith that your words will move that thing and cast it into the ocean? Of course not! If you're going to speak to the mountains in your life, you better have your bathing suit on because you're going to get wet! Most of us ARE our own problem when it comes to faith for the impossible. Most of us are functional atheists. We give the Word of God lip service and generally have a mental assent that certain doctrines are true, but we live our lives as though God doesn't really do what the Word says He does. There's many people who "believe" in divine healing, but I'd never waste my time going to them for prayer if I needed a miracle in my body. Why? Because I know they already have ruled out the possibility anything will happen if they pray, and they would just pray out of respect or to be nice, but not out of the place of being convinced that their prayers bear fruit.

Let's tackle some observations I've made about the text:

- Jesus mentions speaking three times.
- Jesus mentions believing/expecting/having faith a total of three times
- It appears that believing that what one says will come to pass is a prerequisite for it to come to pass.
- The people who can move mountains are the 'whoevers'. I dare to believe this applies to every believer. Are you a whoever?
- Doubting is a pre-requisite for making sure the thing you ask doesn't come to pass.
- Both believing and speaking are necessary to yield the result of the mountain being removed and cast into the sea, and not one aspect over the other.

Speak to the Mountains in Your Life

> *"Now faith is the assurance of things hoped for, the conviction of things not seen."* (Heb 11:1)

How do you have assurance for the things you're hoping for? You find out God's will. How do you find out God's will? You find and meditate on passages of Scripture that deal with the specific mountain you're speaking to. For example, if you need healing, you meditate and study Bible passages dealing with healing. If you are having a hard time believing your needs will be met, you study passages where God promises to feed the sparrow or clothe the lilies (Matt 6:25-34) and remind yourself of what He says He will do. You give yourself assurance by knowing His Word from reading what is written in it. This is one of the key ways you speak to the mountains in your life, and cast them into the sea.

As it says in 1 John 5:14-15,

> *"And this is the confidence that we have toward Him, that if we ask anything according to His will, He hears us. And if we know that He hears us in whatever we ask, we know that* ***we have the requests we have asked****."* (emphasis mine)

The best way to know His will is to read it. The Bible is His will in detail. This passage says we know that we have what we ask IF we're praying according to His will.

> *"But let him ask in faith, with no doubting, for the one who doubts is like a wave of the sea that is driven and tossed by the wind. For that person must not suppose he will receive anything from the Lord; he is a double-minded man, unstable in all his ways."* (James 1:6-8)

Do you have confidence and not doubt in your heart? Faith is knowing it will happen when you have no outward evidence. That's what makes it different than hope. Faith is certain, whereas hope doesn't know for sure what will happen. Also, this part in James here should be used every time someone tells you nobody needs more faith, or that we all have the same amount. If I've heard it or been told it once, I've been told it a thousand times: *"How can you say someone doesn't have enough faith for something?"* Simple: if they have faith for the thing, it will come to pass. However, we must remember that faith requires perseverance.

Most people have an "I-believe-God-could-do-that-and-I-hope-that-He-will" mental assent about God, but that's not faith. Faith requires the tenacity to keep going for it until it happens. Hope begs God to come through, not knowing if

He will or not. Faith is certain that He will with no doubting.

The epistle of James says that if a double-minded man should not expect to receive anything from the Lord, then don't you think the opposite of double-minded, a single-focused man will? If faith is not faith without works (James 2:14-26), then neither is doubt really doubt unless it is accompanied by its corresponding works (actions opposite of faith). Faith requires action for it to be considered faith, and doubt requires action in order for it to be doubt.

I remember not long ago I was reading in the newspaper about a pit bull who was attacking a man. Neighbors came and were beating on the dog and trying to get it to let go of this person's arm. It would not let up and they kept beating on it, and grabbing it, and trying to force it off of the guy it was attacking, but to no avail. Finally someone got a rifle and killed the dog and it still had its teeth sunk into the guy's flesh!

We need to be like pit bulls in believing God and having faith for the impossible, and determine that we're not going to let go of the promises in God's Word until we see them come to pass in our lives. I know that may sound blasphemous to some readers. God has done his part and now it's up to us to persevere and receive. Remember the persistent widow in Luke 18? The first verse says Jesus told them that they ought always to pray and not lose heart. The problem is most of us hardly ever pray, and do often lose heart.

Steve, this stuff sounds really "name it and claim it, blab it and grab it" to me.

I know. But if you want to see an example of believing in your heart and saying with your mouth and believing what you say will come to pass and then having it come to pass that you probably have already done, then remember what the Bible says in Romans 10:9-10:

> *"The word is near you, in your mouth and in your heart" (that is, the word of faith that we proclaim); because, if you **confess with your mouth** that Jesus is Lord **and believe in your heart** that God raised him from the dead, **you will** be saved. For with the heart one believes and is justified, and with the mouth one confesses and is saved."*

Romans 10:9-10 is simply Mark 11:23-24 applied specifically to salvation. The human soul getting born again is the ultimate moving of a mountain! You believe, you speak, and what you believe and speak according to God's will, happens. God's will is for all to be saved (2 Peter 3:9). Therefore someone coming to Him in faith, confessing with their mouth, and believing in their heart, causes them to receive what they are promised by Him because they believed and confessed according to His instruction in the Word about it. You have to meet the conditions of the promise in order to receive the promise, and God would not promise you something if He had no intention of giving it to you when you meet the conditions He lays out.

God is not a respecter of persons (Acts 10:34), which means He doesn't favor one person's request over another or respect them more than you. God won't withhold from you something if He promises it in the Word — that's why it's in there, so you can know what He promises.

> *"God is not a man that He should lie, or a son of man, that He should change His mind. Has he said, and will he not do it? Or has he spoken and will he not fulfill it?"* (Numbers 23:19).

> *"Every good gift and every perfect gift is from above, coming down from the Father of lights with whom there is no variation or shadow due to change."* (James 1:17).

So all believers and followers of Christ reading this — you have already put this principle into practice in your life by initially getting saved. It's just that few of us speak to mountains and believe in our heart they will move when it comes to other areas of our lives. We're afraid we'll be selfish. We're afraid it will work. We're afraid we'll go off into practicing this in weird areas of our lives like cars and big houses like some other ministers do. We're also afraid we won't ask for the right things or that God will say 'no'. He won't say no if you're praying according to the promises in His Word. The promises of God in Him are 'yes' and 'amen' (2 Cor 1:20).

If you get the answer 'no', then either a demon is speaking to you, or you're praying differently than what the Word of God gives you any right to believe for. If you're praying contrary to the Word of God and have no promise from Him to stand on, then you are in presumption or foolishness or both, and I cannot guarantee you what will happen as a result.

That's why constant Bible reading and meditation is important. It renews your mind so you can know what the will of God is. (Romans 12:2)

GROWING DEEPER ROOTS

"Blessed is the man who walks not in the counsel of the wicked, nor stands in the way of sinners, nor sits in the seat of scoffers; but his delight is in the law of the LORD, and on his law he meditates day and night. He is like a tree planted by streams of water that yields its fruit in its season, and its leaf does not wither. In all that he does, he prospers. The wicked are not so, but are like chaff that the wind drives away." (Psalm 1:1-4)

KING DAVID

Any tree, and pretty much all plants and vegetation in general, need several things in order to grow and produce their corresponding fruit: proper soil, water, and sunlight. If you water it too much and/or only give it water, then it will get waterlogged and die. If you don't give it any, and it only gets heat and sunlight, it will die. But the soil also needs to be in correct condition. The parable of the sower (Matthew 13:1-9, 18-23) details the different outcomes of having the seed fall on different types of ground. In Psalm 1 we're given a few contrasts between the righteous and the wicked which I'd like to focus on. The man who delights in the law of the Lord is contrasted with the man who doesn't, but who walks in the counsel of the wicked and sits in the seat of the scornful. In this passage we're told that the man who delights in the law of the Lord and meditates on it day and night is not like a *seed*, but how he's like a **tree** planted by streams of living water. The man of wickedness, like a leaf that withers.

It stands to reason that if the righteous man is the one who grows and prospers it would be necessary to know *how* he does so. Therefore we need to be delighting in the law of the Lord if we're to prosper and be blessed in all areas of righteousness -- through both the *rhema* revelation along the *logos* written Word, studying it, getting into it deep and sinking our roots deep into it. Only from having these conditions in place in our own lives, will we be able to extract the image from the seed, the Word of God. The man who does this yields fruit in season, and in *all* that he does he prospers. It's also necessary to realize that one must to do this *regularly*, as indicated in the words 'day and night'. As the saying goes, an apple a day keeps the doctor away, but not if you *only* eat one apple and nothing else in the course of a day!

Since all Scripture is God-inspired, then the meaning of one passage is tied into the one before it and breeds the meaning of the one following. All the parables, teachings and stories are like the strokes of brush used to develop a much larger painting. All of it ties together. Therefore, passages like Psalm 1 don't require a lot of scholarly study to understand, and if we just read the whole thing in context we can understand the individual verses contained therein. As good as it is to memorize individual Scripture verses, it's even better to meditate on entire chapters of Scripture and entire stories or parables as opposed to individual verses. Doing so helps avoid accidentally or intentionally lifting sentences out of context.

If a blessed man doesn't walk in the counsel of the wicked, and all the things detailed in the first two verses of this Psalm, then that means the unrighteous man does the opposite. If a righteous man is like a tree firmly planted, then a wicked person is not, and if an unrighteous person is not getting his counsel from the law of the Lord, *then by necessity* he's getting his counsel somewhere else. James 3:13-18 explains that the only other alternative is to be getting it from below. And by 'below', I don't mean the ground, but the pit of hell.

We read in passages like Luke 6:43-44 that no good tree bears bad fruit, and vice versa. There's only two options -- good or bad; fruitful or unfruitful, righteous or wicked, good fruit or bad fruit. That which is from below or that which is from above. A wicked person who is not firmly planted near the streams of living water is not going to yield fruit as though he were firmly planted in good soil. Verse 45 goes on to say that the good person out of the good treasure of his heart produces good, and the evil person out of his evil treasure produces evil, for out of the **abundance of the heart the mouth speaks**. Therefore, it's no wonder the very next thing Jesus proceeds to teach here in Luke 6 is about building your house on a rock so that it withstands the storm. The idea of building and construction is linked to sowing, reaping, growing, and harvesting in this context. The fact Luke writes them one immediately following the other in his Gospel allows us to assume they are a part of the same flow of thought Jesus was teaching here.

> *"Everyone who comes to me and hears my words and does them, I will show you what he is like: he is like a man building a house, who **dug deep** and laid the **foundation on the rock**. And when a flood arose, the stream broke against that house and could not shake it, because **it had been well built**. But the **one who hears and does not do them** is like a man who built a house on the ground without a*

foundation. When the stream broke against it, immediately it fell, and the ruin of that house was great." (Luke 6:47-49 emphasis mine)

For years I read that passage of Scripture as though it were talking about the believer and the unbeliever, the righteous versus the unrighteous. However, *both individuals heard*, but only one did what he heard, the other didn't, and the storms and cares of this life knocked the structure down.

So why am I saying all that, and how exactly do we extract the content of the incorruptible seed of Christ in us? Those passages will be a loose framework for us to work with to provide some steps for obtaining revelation knowledge and extracting the image from the seed, which we will spend the rest of this book covering.

Put into practice what you learn from the Word of Christ

This is of the utmost importance in growing in Him and extracting revelation knowledge from the seed. In receiving the implanted word, James 1:21-25 talks of making sure to be doers of the Word of Christ, which would be building your house on the rock, versus being a listener only–building on sandy foundations. One person extracts the image from inside the seed BY obeying what Christ teaches and the other didn't, and the ruin of his house was great.

> "But the one who looks into the perfect law, the law of liberty, and perseveres, being no hearer who forgets but a doer who acts, he **will be blessed in his doing.**" (James 1:25)

Submit to fiery trials in your life

> "Count it all joy, my brothers, when you meet trials of various kinds, for you know that the **testing of your faith produces steadfastness**. And let steadfastness have its full effect, that you may be perfect and complete, lacking in nothing." (James 1:2-4)

Under circumstances like heat and fiery trials in life, we're capable of having squeezed out of us just what's really inside our hearts. It's these moments that reveal our true character. Sometimes the greatest opportunity for our faith to grow, as already mentioned, is from being under pressure. Remember, your faith has no perishing point (1 Peter 1:7).

The light of the sun is vital and is a crucial component to the growth of any vegetation similar to the way muscle doesn't grow except under resistance. But your true, tried, and tested genuine faith will survive the heat, and you will be refined and made purer, and steadfastness is produced in your life the way fruit grows from the tree planted by that stream of living water.

Create the right conditions in your life for the growth

As already mentioned, certain conditions need to be right for the seed to sprout and germinate properly. We see this exact same concept exemplified in the parable of the sower where the same seed is scattered in each instance, but the conditions are different. The seed that sprouted up immediately is the one that withers and dies under the heat–the pressure and trials of life. The soil of our hearts has to be right, or else the seed doesn't go deep and develop any roots. You can't have too much sunlight, and yet you can't have too little either. You can't have too much water, yet you can't have too little. There's a correct balance that's necessary. Likewise, if the soil is too shallow, the roots can't grow deep.

Several years ago, when I was living as a missionary in Holland, some dear Dutch sisters gave me a vetplante for my birthday. I'm not an expert on plants and flowers by any stretch of the imagination, but it had very thick leaves and had an interesting rubber like texture. These sisters gave it to me in a small pot and told me it could go weeks without being watered so that way I wouldn't have to worry about watering it every day or having it die if I forgot about it for a few days. Not only that, but if I put it in a larger bowl or pot, the plant would grow even larger. Such is the case with our lives—we can only dig our roots as deep as how much room we have to grow in, and without deep roots we won't have much fruit to blossom where we're planted.

The phrase *unplowed ground* (NIV) or *fallow ground* (KJV) is soil that could be productive, but has not been broken up, tilled, plowed, and prepared for planting. Unplowed ground won't let a crop grow. It's hard, preventing the seed from penetrating, germinating, and fully growing into its destiny.

Don't fragment the seed

The seed itself also has to be left intact. Nobody who knows a thing or two about farming would take a seed and split it into pieces smaller than it already is, and then sow each piece and expect a bigger harvest. Nor would they expect partial incomplete harvest because none would be obtained. Why? Because the image in the seed would have been destroyed by splitting and dividing it. You can't sow just the part of the seed responsible for leaves, and then just the part of the seed responsible for fruit, and just the part of the seed that will be responsible for wood, and expect to grow any of those components independent of the other. They are all a part of the same package.

Likewise it is with the heavenly seed, the Word of God. We can't add to it or take away from it. We can't split up any of its aspects and over-emphasize one component over the other. *It all works and accomplishes something together.* We sow it as it is. The Holy Spirit will work with the written text of the Bible He authored. It's imperative that we take the whole counsel of the Word of God, and not just select our portions that suit our purposes.

Scripture Memorization

I'm going to take some more time to talk about the power of Scripture memorization because I've always had an affinity for memorizing the Bible. When I was a child and attended daily vacation Bible schools or Christian day camps, we'd receive rewards for memorizing select passages. When I was 17 years old and started volunteering my summers at *Hope Valley Day Camp* a couple of years after I got saved, we were given twelve Bible verses we needed to memorize in order to be ready to share the Gospel with children who wanted to give their lives to Jesus. Memorization was how we were able to know with certainty what the Word of God said concerning salvation and assurance of God's salvation. To this day, I still know the verses we used, even if I struggle to tell you the "address" where they're located.

Other than that, I'd never made much of a habit or routine of memorizing Bible verses on my own as part of my spiritual diet. It wasn't until I had come back from my first year away at Bible College in Pensacola, Florida, and I had a lot of friends who didn't understand speaking in tongues or the Baptism in the Holy Spirit. For this reason I decided to memorize all the verses I learned in one of my classes. I took out my notebook, looked up the references in my Bible and started writing them out on index cards.

One day I decided to do an Internet search about a TV minister who I would rather not name, but is nicknamed in some circles as "the walking Bible." I'll admit, in those days my motives for being able to memorize the Scriptures was so I could quote them like this man did and shut my friends up when they tried arguing with me. I figured I could get the advantage over them by being able to quote the Bible rather than whipping it out and turning to passages in it. God has humbled me a lot over the years and soon after my desire for doing this was to store God's word in my heart (Psalm 119:11), and not to look smart before others.

This particular minister stated that to get full of the Word of God took him decades and he was still memorizing daily well into his seventies. His method was to arrange verses according to Bible doctrine and place them on index cards that he could carry with him. It was a means of converting time spent commuting or waiting, and turning such time into profitable opportunities for storing God's Word in his heart. Since I had just started a job that summer working in a factory standing at a machine all day and taking plastic parts out and inspecting them for defects, I could use something besides the radio to pass the time. I decided to give this a try.

As stated, the first topic I attempted this with was speaking in tongues and the Holy Spirit in general. Copying the preacher, I prepared index cards with Bible verses on one side and the references on the other. Since I was in a season of my life where I'd be spending hours a day at a monotonous job, I prepared about thirty cards, at least. You might not want to make that many. I also encourage you to write them out yourself, and not just buy a nice set of "encouragement cards" from your local Christian bookstore. There's something special — and not to mention cheaper — about doing this yourself and getting God's Word into your heart while you write your own verses out.

Take whatever area you're struggling in and write verses on index cards for this area. For example you might need God to provide finances. For this, look up all the verses and Psalms you can find about God providing. There's a gold mine in

Jesus' sermon on the mount that contains verses about God feeding the sparrows who do nothing to obtain their food, but yet God feeds them every day (Matthew 6:26) and other verses about how we need not be anxious about anything. The constant barrage of the Word of God concentrated on one subject or theme related to your area of struggle will minister to your spirit in a tremendous way. Also, memorizing verses by subject or doctrine is much easier than trying to do it by chapter in order to bring verses to mind when you want to confess the Word of God over your life, which we'll look at later in this book.

To find the pertinent verses on the theme you want to memorize about, use a good concordance, possibly Strong's or visit Biblegateway.com and make a list of choice verses on the particular word or subject you wish to study. When I first started doing this I chose various charismatic subjects like speaking in tongues and divine healing, as well as other themes or subjects that were of interest to me. Initially starting this habit took many hours of my time looking up the references and writing them out on individual cards. However, since I've always been in the habit of marking up my Bible with different colored pens and highlighters based on subjects, compiling the verses I wanted to use was not a big challenge for me.

Once compiled and written out, I'd read each verse out loud while waiting for a cycle to finish on the machine at the workstation at my job. I'd read the verse just once and wait for the next time the door to that machine would open. Then, when it would spit out the plastic product I needed to inspect, I'd throw it away or make the necessary modifications to it, and then depending on how fast I was at this, I'd have anywhere between 20-30 seconds to wait until the door would open again. You can imagine how Scripture memorization came in handy to pass the time.

Of course, sharing with you how I did this is only meant to be a guideline or to give you ideas. But let me tell you, I wound up looking forward to going to work at my boring job because I was getting revelation, and insight would hit me as I re-read the Word of God out loud. I'd do this for a few hours of my eight-hour shift, and the other part of the day I'd listen to anointed preaching tapes of ministers rightly dividing the word of truth. I did this all throughout the summer of 2002 and I don't regret it one bit. Once I went back to school the next year, it was very difficult to find hours every day to be diligent about this again.

Over time I obviously wouldn't need to keep memorizing verses once I had them committed to memory. Following this method, I'd read each verse out loud seven times, and then put the card at the bottom of the stack. Then, I'd read the next verse seven times, and I'd repeat the process. Then, over time I'd start introducing new verses into my stack and phasing out old ones as I'd learned them.

The minister I learned this from recommended quoting each verse in the first bunch out loud, seven times daily for one week. Then during the second week this can be cut down to twice each day. By the third week once daily was usually sufficient for me. Eventually as I was familiar with the verses I'd start removing them and throwing them away or leaving them lying around for others to find them. You will obviously learn some verses faster than others and you don't have to rigidly follow this pattern, it's just a practical step you can put to use in your life as you increase your faith. I'd never try memorizing any of them all in just one day, though. I'd read the verse seven times out loud, and move on and not touch it again until I got to it the next day.

Since I wasn't able to keep up this habit at this pace when I was no longer working that job, my memorization habits have ebbed and flowed over the years. However, I consider my foundation and knowledge of the word of God to be direct fruit of memorization and extended periods of time praying in tongues. While I lived in the Netherlands, I got back into this habit again when I'd ride the subway quite frequently in the city of Rotterdam, sometimes 30-45 minutes daily. Listening to preaching on my iPod or memorizing Scriptures was the way I'd redeem that time.

You may think to yourself you don't have time in your daily routine to incorporate Scripture memorization on such an extensive scale, but let me ask you, do you have the Internet on your smartphone? If so, checking social media and other time wasters can be easily erased out of your life and focused on something else like this instead.

Don't use a Bible app, but write the verses out. Copying and pasting just doesn't do what writing this out with your own hand and saying it out loud with your own voice will do. At the time of writing this, I still don't have more than a mere WiFi connection on my phone, and I certainly don't have a Facebook phone app because I just can't think of any reason I *need* to know the instant something on social media happens. I can check those things on my laptop when I'm at home.

Listen to Bible mp3s, Preaching and Audio Books

This is not a must, but is a good suggestion if you have a long commute to work or school, or you just don't have the kind of time in your daily routine to be able to read and memorize Scripture. Instead you could use such time in your routine to listen to books of the Bible on mp3. There are websites where you can obtain them freely and legally, or you could check your local Christian bookstore. Once during a visit to Canada I was able to pick up a set of the entire English Standard Version of the Bible on mp3 CDs for only $20. To me, this is a wonderful and inexpensive investment. Now, I have many from ChristianAudio.com and Audible.com

I've gone seasons of my life where I'd put on a book of the Bible, particularly a New Testament epistle such as Romans, or Hebrews, or 1 John and play it on repeat or loop nearby while I slept. Since I'm a light sleeper and sometimes can't fall asleep immediately, I found this a good way to pump stuff into my spirit during those moments.

Have you ever heard or used the expression "sleep on it"? For example, when you need to make an important decision, or maybe some stressful situation or circumstances are bothering you and you feel the urge to deal with it immediately, but instead, you postpone making any rash decisions until you are able to get a good night's sleep, or possibly a decent nap during the day. Good sleep has prevented me from hastily making rash decisions and taking bad actions.

There's something interesting that happens in the moments when we're dozing off to sleep that I believe the Holy Spirit is more free to insert something into our consciousness because we don't have too many thoughts and preoccupations preventing us from hearing His still small voice, and our resistance is relaxed. It's an easier opportunity for him to speak some things to us or impress something on us. It's for this reason I like either reading a book or listening to spiritual audio files of some kind in the final waking moments of my day. I listen to something on my laptop — or headphones on my smartphone or tablet now that I'm married and my wife doesn't like the noise.

Thomas Edison, one of the greatest inventors of the last few centuries and a notoriously sleep deprived "napper" understood something about this. He credited his naps with recharging his imaginative batteries to work on creative problems. He'd sit up in a chair which made it more difficult for him to fully sleep but yet stay lightly conscious. He would hold a steel ball bearing in each hand, and on the floor directly below his closed hand would be a metal saucer. When he fell completely asleep, his hands would relax and each ball bearing would fall onto the metal saucer, making a noise loud enough to wake him up.

Edison utilized what is called hypnagogia, which is a variety of states that can be experienced as we hang onto consciousness while moving towards sleep. It involves bodily relaxation and the easing of the grip of one's cognitive focus. In this state we get the benefit of a sort of emotional and cognitive wandering, or subconscious insights. Edison used this to his creative advantage. Likewise in a negative way this is why cults do their best to keep their adherents sleep deprived so they're more impressionable and easier to manipulate. I figure the positive benefit of this state of consciousness would be to pump truth into my inner man at those barely awake moments before dosing off.

So, make sure to get a good night's sleep and ensure that you're well rested! Don't let worry keep you from resting in the Lord.

Along with listening to Bible mp3s, you can also search for the podcasts of ministers of the Gospel who teach and preach on subjects you need to be built up in or want to learn more about. It's my preference to listen to people who expound a lot on the Scriptures, and not just listen to men and women who share motivational messages, which, though encouraging can also be light on any significant substance. You want to get fed, not just receive a light snack or some cotton candy that doesn't fill you. These light motivational messages may help encourage you in your faith while listening to them, but I highly encourage you to select people who spend a significant amount of time helping you dig into the Bible in their messages. Good enough messages and preaching that will ensure that listening to them repeatedly is beneficial and you'll still be able to get something out of it each time.

You can also get audiobooks but I find these to be rather cost prohibitive compared to buying an audio Bible for the fact that you may be paying the same price for one audiobook with ten hours worth of content as you can pay for hundreds of hours out of the Word of God on your iPod or mobile phone.

If you'd like to get audiobooks, ChristianAudio.com has a membership that includes getting credits to use towards purchasing books, as well as a newsletter subscription that notifies subscribers of free audiobooks of the month. I've been on this list for several years now and have gotten my hands on some very good content. You can also get a membership with Audible.com using your Amazon account. Audible likewise has a credits system where you basically can get a free audiobook per month and a 30% discount on books you purchase. A credit can be used to purchase audiobooks as cheap as $4.99 or audio Bibles that regularly cost $49.99. I have been a customer for nearly 5 years at the time of re-editing this book.

Confess and Speak the Word

To repeat what we talked about earlier, Luke 6:45 states that out of the abundance of the heart the mouth speaks. There's a correlation between what someone believes & thinks in their heart, and what they choose to speak out. Simply put, confession is a statement of your beliefs.

> *"Be filled with the Spirit, **addressing** one another in psalms and hymns and spiritual songs, **singing** and making melody to the Lord with your heart, **giving thanks** always and for everything to God the Father in the name of our Lord Jesus Christ."* (Ephesians 5:18b-20, emphasis mine)

What are you saying with your mouth? If you're storing the Word of God in your heart, you're off to a good start in terms of stuff that you'll be able to pull out of it and confess with your mouth based on both Scripture you may have memorized and from the Holy Spirit having something inside you to draw upon.

I want to spend a moment doing a cursory Scripture study on the importance of the words we speak. Confession has a real bad rap due to some silly and flaky teachings, and abuse and misuse. But there really is a profound truth to being careful of what we speak and say. I notice this kind of teaching is not something noncharismatic/evangelicals really teach a lot on other than token messages or devotionals on '*the power of life and death lies in the tongue*' teaching from Proverbs and of James chapter 3. Charismatics and Pentecostals on the other hand have been known sometimes to go a little too far off with positive confession that the subject has left a bad taste in some peoples' mouths and, in this author's opinion, has been "over corrected."

INCREASE YOUR FAITH

The Bible says in Matthew 12:34b-37:

> *For out of the abundance of the **heart** the **mouth** speaks. The good person out of his good treasure brings forth good, and the evil person out of his evil treasure brings forth evil. I tell you, on the day of judgment people will give account for every careless word they speak, for by your **words** you will be justified, and by your **words** you will be condemned.* (emphasis mine)

It's worth noting the correlation that exists between what someone *believes* and thinks in their heart, and what they choose to *speak* out. If you read the book of Proverbs for more than 10 minutes, you will notice that many of the comparison and contrast proverbs involve speaking. *"The wise man says this, but the fool says that"* over and over again. I've noticed when trying to memorize Scripture verses, that repeating the words in some of those verses I'd written down on little cards helps tremendously. Solomon's Proverbs mention over and over again the *mouth* interchangeably with the *heart* or *thoughts*. I've highlighted texts in my Bibles over the years using specific colored highlighter pens. I usually use different colors to represent different themes or subjects. In one Bible I used blue for passages about what we speak with our mouth. The result is that there's a lot of blue all over the Psalms and wisdom books of the Bible, and some places of the New Testament where I find passages on words, speaking, and meditating.

It astounds me how much there is in the Word of God on this subject, and virtually nobody teaches it other than certain denominations and groups. We hear a lot about how we're to edify and encourage *others* with our words. I'm not against this, but it doesn't end there.

Let's take a cursory look at some passages where I've emboldened some words and phrases for emphasis:

> *"I will **praise** you, O Lord with all my heart, **I will tell of** all your wonders."* (Psalm 9:1)

> *"Lord, who may dwell in your sanctuary? Who may live on your holy hill? He whose walk is blameless, and does what is righteous, who **speaks the truth from his heart** and has **no slander on his tongue**, who does his neighbor no wrong and **casts no slur on his fellowman.**"* (Psalm 15:1-3)

> *"Therefore my **heart** is glad, and my **tongue** rejoices."* (Psalm 16:9)

> *"May the **words** of my mouth and the **meditation** of my **heart** be pleasing in your sight, O Lord, my Rock, and my Redeemer."* (Psalm 19:14)

*"The fool **says** in his **heart** there is no God..."* (Psalm 53:1)

We are told in Psalm 66:1-3a

> *"**Shout** with joy to God, all the earth! **Sing** the glory of his name; make his praise glorious! **Say** to God, "How awesome are your deeds!"*

The psalmist said,

> *"I will sing of the Lord's great love forever; **with my mouth** I will make your faithfulness known through all generations. I will **declare** that your love stands firm forever, that you established your faithfulness in heaven."* (Psalm 89:1-2)

The writer didn't say I "will sing in my head". The psalmist didn't say "I will *think* your praises and hope people telepathically figure out I love you." No, there was *speaking* involved.

> *"Even **in your thought**, do not curse the king, nor in your bedroom curse the rich, for a bird of the air will **carry your voice**, or some winged creature tell the matter."* (Ecclesiastes 10:20).

Again, we see the writer weaving in and out of thoughts and speaking out loud to demonstrate that it's necessary to be careful what we are thinking, because we could accidentally say it out loud and suffer consequences.

One time in a class of mine at Bible school, the teacher was praising the good work that someone on staff had done in a certain area. He asked us all to say something positive to her, or let her know how much we all appreciate her, and to bless her with a word of encouragement. Then, oddly, someone sitting near me very loudly added, "Yeah, bless her with a brick!" The saying "bless 'em with a brick" was jokingly understood in our circle as a way of asking the Lord to deal with someone we didn't like much and drop a brick on their head for us.

It then became obvious that this brother had no idea he said that out loud, but the whole class heard it and the professor said, *"and we'll just ignore that comment and some of us can check our hearts."* It was awkward as this classmate realized he blurted an inner personal thought out loud to his embarrassment! I know I've done the same thing many times.

In my adolescence in Canada, there used to be a series of ads run on TV for a brand of nacho chips, and each commercial followed the same pattern; someone would be waiting in the checkout aisle to make their purchase, and then fade into imagination or day dreaming about a party or something they were looking forward to doing later. Then, they'd yell something out loud, and the commercial would cut back to them standing in line, realizing they were not at their party, but in a grocery store and with everybody looking at them weird for their outburst. The desires of their heart were revealed in a humorous way. What we say reveals what's stored in our heart.

Jesus, **full** of the Word (*being* the Word Himself) quoted Scripture when the devil came and tempted Him (Matthew 4:4, 7, 10). He also told his disciples the things that come out of the mouth come from the heart, and that's what can make a person unclean. *"For out of the heart come evil thoughts, murder, adultery, sexual immorality, theft, false testimony, slander."* (Matthew 15:18-19). It's for this reason alone that I have no respect for Christians using their mouth to cuss, since many words we use as swear words are based on actions of immorality - - and we're not to speak of what the ungodly do in secret (Ephesians 5:12). I don't care if something the apostle Paul said here or there was like cussing in his language in his day — most Christians who justify cussing do it for shock value, and usually in an immature way, or they are just immature in their use of vocabulary. I know I'm meddling with some readers, but deal with it — we're called to be people of excellence in deed and speech.

In closing of this chapter, I'd like to remind you of a few passages about guarding our heart and watching what we speak.

Proverbs 4:23-24 says to *"keep your **heart** with all vigilance, for from it flow the springs of life. Put away from you **crooked speech**, and put devious talk far from you."*

And Ephesians 4:29: *"Let no corrupting talk come out of your mouths, but only such as is good for building up, as fits the occasion, that it may give grace to those who hear"*.

In the final chapter, we will address confession further.

UNDERSTANDING CONFESSION

The Scriptures say a lot on the topic of confession but we're too afraid of diving into it because we're afraid we'll get flaky. I hope you realize I'm *not* talking about standing in your empty garage and confessing you have 5 limousines. I'm not saying I stand in front of a mirror, and put one hand on my head and say, "*I have a full head of hair*", all the while oblivious to the reality that I am in fact, bald. I'm talking about confessing the Word of God over our problems, lives, and circumstances.

"Very few Christians actually realize the place that confession holds in God's scheme of things. Unfortunately, whenever the word 'confession' is used, many invariably think of confessing sins, weaknesses, and failures. That is the negative side of confession. There is however, a positive side of confession, which the Bible has more to say about than the negative.

Webster's dictionary defines "confession" not only as a confession of sins, but as a 'statement of one's beliefs; especially those of the Christian faith.' That is why true Christianity throughout the centuries has been known as 'The Great Confession." Webster's dictionary also defines 'confessor' as "a Christian who has suffered for his faith." The apostles and early fathers of the faith were "bold confessors" of the Word of God."[1]

Simply put, confession is a statement of your beliefs. So what are you saying with your mouth?

> "And they conquered him [the devil] by the blood of the lamb **and** by the **word of their testimony**." (Revelation 12:11)

When I volunteered at a day camp as a counselor in my adolescence during summers off, the leaders made us volunteers memorize passages of Scripture referred to as 'salvation verses' and 'assurance verses', so we would be able to show kids who wanted to give their lives to Jesus passages in the Bible that showed them how. I say that as a way of indicating I know many Christians, even in evangelical circles, that already know what confession is in a sense.

Again, merely believing only does so much. Speaking is directly tied to what you believe. Out of the abundance of the heart the mouth speaks. In fact, it takes just this one verse in Romans to show the idea that "we don't need to talk about our faith, but just *live* it out" is a pile of rubbish. Just looking in the Scriptures shows our faith is of necessity demonstrated by the words of our mouth, our confession.

For those who think it's not necessary to say anything about the reason for your hope, Jesus said in Matthew 10:32-33: "So everyone who *acknowledges* me before men, I also will acknowledge before my Father who is in heaven, *but whoever denies me before men, I also will deny before my Father who is in heaven.*" Is there any other way to acknowledge Christ before men *without* words? Very little. With most communication in real life interaction, you can only learn what someone thinks by what they say and talk about, and not by observing their body language alone.

Re-read the above Bible passages carefully even if you think you know this stuff already — it's foundational. Just because something is basic and elementary doesn't mean we don't need to be reminded of it now and again. Chew on them. Literally.

Pray in Tongues & Allow the Holy Spirit to work Through You

In my recent book *Nine Lies People Believe About Speaking in Tongues*, I cover tongues as an aspect of building oneself up in the faith in more detail than I'm about to here. As such, I encourage you to read that book for further elaboration. However, I couldn't talk about increasing your faith and not include something about the powerful role of praying in the Holy Spirit. And so we will conclude the book with this practice.

Jesus said *'Whoever believes in me, as the Scripture has said, 'Out of his heart will flow rivers of living water.'* (John 7:38) He was talking about the Holy Spirit, who "waters" this seed — the Word of God in us, and supplies the power to bring it to fruition. All that you need to live holy and grow in Christ is contained in that seed. The Holy Spirit will work with the written text of the Bible He authored.

In John 14:17, Jesus said the Holy Spirit will be with us AND in us. These are two different things. The Holy Spirit is with us *corporately* as a body of believers, and He's with the *individual* believer on the inside of us. He builds up the Church, and He builds up the individual believer.

In 1 Corinthians 3:16, Paul tells the church at Corinth that collectively as a church they are the temple of the Holy Spirit. Not every Bible translation makes that obvious. The Amplified translation brings out that the church is the temple of the Holy Spirit collectively, and the individual is the temple of the Holy Spirit individually. Compare this with 1 Corinthians 6:19, where we're told our body is a temple of the Holy Spirit.

This is also part of the reason why when believers are baptized in the Holy Spirit sometime after their salvation experience, there are different varieties of the gift of tongues available to them. Each version of the Holy Spirit's "temple" has this phenomena manifested. In the corporate setting the Holy Spirit distributes gifts freely as He sees fit, but we can seek after and desire to operate in some more than others for the benefit of the *rest of the Church Body*. One person can have the public corporate version of the gift of tongues, and another believer the interpretation (in a public setting). It's true — not every believer has the *corporate* version of the gift of tongues. This is what I believe Paul was referring to — the local church setting — when he asked in 1 Corinthians 12:30 "*do all speak with tongues? Do all interpret?*"

However, every gift of the Holy Spirit that operates collectively in the body of Christ has an "individual" version for the believer. All may prophesy (1 Cor. 14:31), all believers can/may speak in tongues (Mark 16:17), anyone who believes may lay hands on the sick (Mark 16:18), and so on. When you're not around other believers, do you refuse to operate in a spiritual gift because you don't think it's the one you have? Of course not! But corporately, in meetings like Church services, Bible studies, and home meetings, someone else will be the one to demonstrate certain giftings instead of us.

The Role of This 'Confession' in Personal Revelation & Edification

First Corinthians 14:4 says that when someone speaks in tongues, that the person who speaks in an unknown tongue edifies himself. The word edify comes from the Greek work *oikodomeo* which means to build a house or erect a building. It literally means to build upward, especially a skyline, or to top out a building or structure. An edifier is one who plans, designs or constructs such edifices. It follows then that the more we understand what edification is, then we understand this process of edifying ourselves literally has to do with renovating, improving and strengthening the foundations of our 'temple' of the Holy Spirit so to speak. As we yield to the Holy Spirit, He will build into us the revelation of everything Christ is in us, our hope and glory, and build into us the character of Christ.

That being said, there's the gift of tongues that edify the *collective* temple of the Holy Spirit (see 1 Corinthians 14: 5, and 22), and there's a tongue that edifies the *individual* Holy Spirit temples. First Corinthians 14:4, and 13-17 go into a bit of detail on this, and Romans 8:26-7 speaks of intercessional groanings and *'praying when we know not what we ought to pray'*. As I elaborate on in my other book on tongues, there are two types of the gift of tongues for the corporate gathering of believers, for their benefit and edification, and one of them is accompanied by an interpretation. The tongue could be a natural language.

The other two types of the gift of tongues are for the individual believer on a more personal level, which is what we're focused on for our personal edification process, or, building ourselves up in our faith (see Jude 20). The interpretation comes in the form of revelation and/or strength in the believer's spirit. Every believer can benefit from this personal use of tongues, but misunderstanding and lack of familiar experience are the main inhibitor preventing many evangelicals from entering into this realm of the Holy Spirit, which is why I took the time to focus on many of those misconceptions in a separate book.

As mentioned, the gift for personal use is something that every believer can have following the baptism in the Holy Spirit. Each instance the baptism in the Holy Spirit is talked about in the book of Acts, the manifestation of other tongues accompanied it, and in Acts 19, prophecy did also. Both are revelation/edification tools that involve *speaking* something.

Keeping in mind the framework we've established on the role of confession in watering the seed of our faith, the "confession" that accompanies the baptism in the Holy Spirit, is the gift of tongues for personal edification. I have decided to use the term "inner-fortification [of the inner man]" interchangeably with "edification", but you'll see that's naturally what I mean by that.

The Holy Spirit Doesn't Have A Memory Problem

When John tells us the Holy Spirit will teach us ALL things, the disciples — who were the ones being spoken to here — didn't have all of Jesus' words written down in a Bible yet for the Holy Spirit to bring revelation from. Jesus was not telling them the Holy Spirit would help them memorize the *Romans Road* or the *Sermon on the Mount*. They had to rely on the Holy Spirit bringing to remembrance what He had *told them personally* — not from mental or spiritual recollection of the Bible *merely* as a living text. The disciples had the Word Himself, Jesus Christ, in their midst for 3 ½ years to learn from *personally*. However, 2000 years later, since we did not have that exact same experience as them, it's not a misinterpretation to take this text to say the Holy Spirit brings life to the *written* Word for us this way.

The very first few verses of the book of Genesis mention how the Spirit of the Lord was hovering over the face of the waters. He was involved when God *spoke* the Word and brought forth life and all therein. The Psalms mention how God knew us before He formed us in the womb. Before we ever set foot on the face of the earth and began to speak some goo-goos and ga-gas, the Lord had a plan for your individual life. *That* is what the Holy Spirit brings to remembrance in us as we pray in tongues! The Holy Spirit — Who is living in you if you're a believer — repeats to you and gives you revelation and insight into the things God has spoken and decreed about your life before the foundation of the world, and Holy Spirit helps build you up and qualify you *into* that plan/God's will. God has a perfect will for us that we can miss. He has set up in His unending wisdom a way to deposit that will on the inside of us, and then let us unpack at our pace, through praying in tongues — edifying ourselves in the spirit, and growing in our faith as a result.

In that same chapter of John, Jesus was not exclusively talking about the words of Jesus He spoke 2000 years ago - the Holy Spirit is capable of remembering words spoken no matter how long ago they were spoken. He is not bound by time like we are. Everything that ever has happened or will happen has already happened and not yet happened, in a manner of speaking, from His point of view already. The moment that He was hovering over the waters in Genesis 1:2 and the moment He speaks of in Revelation 22:17 inviting the Lord Jesus to come back are on the same level plane in the history of existence.

Am I shaking your brain yet? This stuff is hard for us finite beings to understand since we're linear and bound by time. The Spirit of God takes the things He has heard about your life and the plan God has for it, and reveals them to you. The fact of the matter is that the Holy Spirit, according to Jesus, takes what He has *heard*, and repeats it or makes it known to us.

When and where exactly did the Holy Ghost *hear* things to tell us? Well friend, did you know this includes things that are not "written in the Book"? This includes the calling God has for you. This includes whom you'll marry. This includes what you should do today. But, my friend, Holy Spirit is never going to contradict what He has allowed to be written down in this book we call the Bible. The Author of that Book is never going to give you revelation that contradicts the Book He Himself penned through human hands! Remember, the Spirit and the Word are one (1 John 5:7). If you ever hear someone teaching some "new teaching" that they say God revealed to them, ask them for at least three Scripture passages to back it up!

Steve, what on earth does this revelation stuff and speaking in tongues have to do with building up my faith?

I've been going a bit down another path but I'm now coming around full circle as we conclude in order to say that extended tongue praying is directly related to personal edification and revelation — and inner fortification. I'm just saying all this stuff to get you jealous to be doing it more in your life if you're not already. Slowly or speedily, it's up to us — the same way an athlete decides how much time he's going to spend in the gym working out and developing his muscles. God doesn't sovereignly "ordain" him to just get buff overnight. The athlete is in charge of how much he's going to do this practice, and likewise every believer is a steward of their own spiritual edification. Speaking and praying in the Holy Spirit is a tremendous aid in watering the seed of our faith and helping us strengthen our roots deeper.

Be blessed, and may God draw you into deeper and deeper realms of His Spirit.

1. Bob and Rose Weiner, Bible Studies for a Firm Foundation, (Maranatha Publications Inc., 1985 p. 85)

ABOUT THE AUTHOR

Steve Bremner is a missionary to Peru and a *FIRE School of Ministry* graduate. He has a burden for grounding people in the Word of God and seeing believers from all sorts of backgrounds live out and experience the power of the Holy Spirit, and the love of God in their lives and ministries.

Steve also thinks it's pretentious when authors and bloggers write their own bio pages but refer to themselves in the third person.

I — I mean *he* — served in the Netherlands for almost 2 years before moving to South America. The gift of teaching and a pastoral heart are what characterize Steve's calling, and in Peru so far he's had opportunities to teach in a local seminary, share the love of Christ to some of the underprivileged, and traveled to shanty towns outside of Lima, the nation's capital, to teach with and serve alongside other established ministries. He is now living in Chorrillos, and is part of a missional community called *Oikos,* and teaches full time in its school of ministry.

Steve is Canadian (and is not ashamed of it), and was sent out by *River Run Fellowship,* located in Peterborough, Ontario. That's in Canada, for those who need it clarified. If it weren't for his home fellowship, and its lead elder Stephen Best, he would never have gone to Peru where he is beginning to see God do things he once only imagined and daydreamed about.

Like any other author, Steve and Lili are using the proceeds from their online book sales to finance their disciple-making in Peru. One way you can support them that doesn't require any of your money is by leaving a rating and writing a review of this book on sites where it can be downloaded.

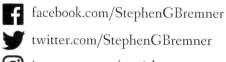

facebook.com/StephenGBremner
twitter.com/StephenGBremner
instagram.com/steviebremner

FIRE ON YOUR HEAD PODCAST

If the Internet had been available to the Apostle Paul, he'd have used it make the Word of God available to as many people as he could. For this reason, Steve co-hosts and produces the *Fire On Your Head* podcast, which can be subscribed to in Apple Podcasts and other popular podcatcher programs such as Stitcher Radio, Spotify and Google Podcasts.

You can visit the site directly at www.fireonyourhead.com.

ALSO BY STEVE BREMNER

9 LIES PEOPLE BELIEVE ABOUT SPEAKING IN TONGUES

Crushing myths and fallacies about the wonderful gift God gives freely

Have you ever believed or been told that speaking in tongues is not for today? Or do you believe that it is for today, but not for everybody, or that its contemporary use is suspicious?

These are some of the most common misconceptions people have about this particular gift of the Holy Spirit. In this book, Steve Bremner Scripturally answers these and other objections to modern-day glossolalia.

Other objections covered in this book include:

- "Tongues are not for today."
- "Holy Spirit baptism already happened at salvation."
- "Speaking in tongues is the least important of the spiritual gifts."
- "You aren't supposed to speak in tongues unless there's an interpreter."
- "You can't just speak in tongues at will."

This book will help you destroy the traditions of man and the lies of religion that nullify the power of God in your life. Begin a new love walk and experience depths in God you never knew were possible through praying in tongues.

Get your Kindle version on Amazon for only $9.99 (click here) or get the paperback version for only $15.99 (click here)

THE IMPERISHABLE SEED OF CHRIST

Understanding the Believer's Spiritual DNA

"Having purified your souls by your obedience to the truth for a sincere brotherly love, love one another earnestly from a pure heart, since you have been born again, not of perishable seed but of imperishable, through the living and abiding word of God." 1 Peter 1:22-23

What is this imperishable seed with which we've been born again? All flesh is like grass and the things of this world will fade away. In this short but rich book Steve Bremner challenges you to live a life that is "imperishable" and will survive the transition into the age to come while the things of this world, pass away.

This book is also an exploration of the parable of the sower and the principles of reproduction in the Kingdom of God, focusing primarily on Christ's imagery and language about the seed in the parable of the sower, as well as Paul's construction metaphors in his first letter to the Corinthians.

Get the Kindle version on Amazon for only $2.99 (click here)

SIX LIES PEOPLE BELIEVE ABOUT DIVINE HEALING

The Truth About God's Will to Heal the Sick

Have you ever believed God had made you sick to teach you a lesson?

Do you believe God wants some to be sick but others to be well for a divine purpose known only to Himself?

Have you struggled with a healing in your body or spirit but it seemed as though God just doesn't want to answer your prayers for healing

Do you believe you've got a thorn in the flesh God is using to refine your character?

These are lies, and Steve Bremner Scripturally and carefully answers these objections to healing along with other misconceptions that many Christians believe when it comes to divine healing.

This quick read will help you destroy the traditions of man and lies of religion that nullify the power of God in your life!

What we believe about God and how He works can have a dramatic impact on how we approach Him and what we expect of Him. Many Christians believe lies about The Father that keep them bound and prevent healing in their bodies and in their lives.

In his conversational style, Steve helps you learn what some of the top lies are that hold Christians and unbelievers back when it comes to divine healing. You too can receive healing and heal the sick.

Quit believing lies today. God is not just "able" to heal, He is *willing!*

If you'd like to give a copy to a Spanish-speaking friend, give them a copy of **6 Mentiras Que Las Personas Creen Sobre La Sanidad Divina**.

Buy either digital version for only $4.99 on Amazon

GET THESE BONUSES WHEN YOU BUY OUR AUDIOBOOK

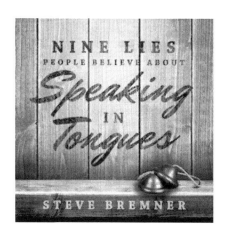

9 Lies People Believe About Speaking in Tongues is finally available in audiobook format

Have you ever been told that speaking in tongues is "not for today?'

Maybe you've heard people speak in tongues... and it seemed weird. You thought to yourself, *"This is too strange to be God!"*

Or, maybe you believe that people can still speak in tongues today... but it's not for everybody.

Whether you're skeptical or intrigued, whether you speak in tongues or don't, this book is for you!

In Nine Lies People Believe About Speaking in Tongues, I biblically confront myths about speaking in tongues head-on and answer some of the most common questions about this controversial spiritual gift.

But wait — there's more!

If you buy a copy of the audiobook on Audible, Amazon, iTunes or wherever you can *legitimately* get it, I'll send you 7 bonus mp3s from Brian Parkman, mentor of mine and co-writer of two of the chapters. These files he's given me permission to give away are teachings he offered in recent years on the following:

- **2 classes** of *The More Excellent Way* (see 1 Corinthians 13)
- **5 classes** of *Practicing and Imparting Spirit Baptism*

Each class on average is between 60-75 minutes long, making this upwards of 7 hours of bonus content, and perfect for those of you wanting to understand the dynamics of the various types of the gift of speaking in tongues. You'll also learn to minister the baptism to other people and help them understand it better, along with other really cool stuff that has personally had a big impact on me and my relationship with the Holy Spirit.

All of this for only $14.95 (or $9.95 if you're already an AudibleListener) and if you read to the end I'll tell you how to **get it free**!

Why Audio?

I know you're a smart cookie who knows how to read. You got this far didn't you? Audio means you can learn on the go. While driving or commuting, working out at the gym or while doing chores like giving your dog a bath. There have been studies that have shown that we need to **_hear_ something at least three times before we can really grab hold** and run with the information. Reading works too, but how many of us will read a book three times? Listening three times is a breeze. When you lead someone into a Holy Spirit baptism, you need the "how" engrained. You need to not be flipping through a book looking up the info.

Sound good? Ok, here's how you get it!

If you purchase the audiobook from audibletrial.com/fireonyourhead and forward me your receipt or your order confirmation — anything digital or scanned proving you legitimately got the audiobook — to **fireonyourhead (AT) stevebremner (DOT) com**, I'll personally send you a link with all the bonus downloads.

If you join Audible's 30 day trial, you'll be given a credit that can be used toward the book allowing you to get it for free. You can forward me your order confirmation even if you didn't pay for the book but simply used the free credit you got with your 30 day free trial.

If you already have the Kindle version or you want to read it as well, you can get the Audible Narration added for only $7.49 as well. When buying the Kindle book on Amazon, you'll see the option to add Audible narration when purchasing the book.

That Audible membership will be a handy time saver for all of the things you want to learn, although you can cancel your membership when your 30 days are up and still keep the audiobook long after.

Rules/Terms/Conditions/The Fine Print/Things You Should Know

- I check this email account once every 24 hours daily. Please be patient if you don't hear from me immediately.
- Prices presented to you by Audible or Amazon may be different from listener to listener, based on various things such as whether you're already an Audible listener or a new one, and geographical location while browsing the web.
- You CAN purchase the book on Amazon or iTunes and forward me that receipt. However, you will only be able to start a free 30 day trial (and obtain the audiobook free) on Audible.

PARTNER WITH US AS MISSIONARIES

If you were touched by this book and would like to make a donation to sow directly into Steve and Lili Bremner on the mission field in Peru, please follow these instructions:

In the USA:
Make checks payable to:
WORLD OUTREACH CENTER
PO Box 3478,
Fort Mill, SC 29708

Please Indicate it's for The Bremners /Peru

Visit their site to donate online: www.worldoutreachcommunity.org

STEVE BREMNER

Thank you for your encouragement and support.

Made in the USA
Monee, IL
15 December 2021